WHY DOCTRINES?

WHY
DOCTRINES?

CHARLES C. HEFLING, JR.

Lines from "Church Going" by Philip Larkin are reprinted by permission of St. Martin's Press; copyright The Marvell Press, 1955, 1960.

International Standard Book No.: 0-936384-09-3
Library of Congress Catalog No.: 82-83553

Published in the United States of America by Cowley Publications.

Cover design by James Madden, SSJE.

To
BERNARD LONERGAN
teacher, colleague, friend
in his eightieth
year

Preface

Having said in the first chapter something about where
this book comes from and where it is going, all I have left to say
here is a word of thanks.

First, to Cynthia Shattuck, who knew perfectly well what
editing a book of mine would entail, and did it anyway. How
much these pages owe to her patient persistence and deft judgment is probably more than I know, and what I know is more
than I can easily say.

Then, to Fred Lawrence, Joseph Flanagan, and Patrick Byrne.
Thinking is conversation, and it has been my joy to take part
with them, jointly and severally, in an ongoing conversation that
has changed my thinking, about this book and a great deal more,
by changing me.

Finally, to a philosopher and theologian whose name appears
only once or twice but whose ideas will be evident, to those who
know his work, on nearly every page. With deep gratitude and
affection, I have dedicated the book to him.

CHARLES C. HEFLING, JR.

Boston College
25 February 1984

CONTENTS

❦ ONE ❦
Why Doctrines?

---

*Let it be remembered then, that religion comes under the twofold considera-
tion of internal and external: for the latter is as real a part of religion, of true
religion, as the former.*

JOSEPH BUTLER

QUESTIONS COME BEFORE answers. Whatever we under-
stand, we first wonder about. If we are indeed rational animals, it
is because we are in the first place inquisitive animals, endowed
with an urge or appetite for knowledge that arises unbidden and
takes shape in questions. It is our most distinctively human
privilege. Like cows and canaries, we can gaze at things, but we
can also understand what we are gazing at, because they do not
take the first step towards knowledge and we do. We ask questions. That is how every investigation starts.

The priority of questions to answers is a theme that will recur
frequently in the pages that follow. It also lies behind the strategy
of the book as a whole. For every investigation not only starts
with a question but also takes its direction from the *kind* of
question it starts with. Take kangaroos, for instance. It makes a
difference whether you tackle this subject in the way German
professors are said to favor—"prolegomena to some introductory
considerations of the question whether and to what extent the
kangaroo belongs to the category of mammals"—or instead adopt
a more pragmatic approach and begin at once with the question,
"Can the kangaroo carry passengers?" The same thing holds for
the question that gives this investigation its title: by explaining
what I mean by 'Why doctrines?' I will also be introducing the
book.

It might seem that the German professorial method, though somewhat pedantic, has a point, namely that important terms need to be defined at the outset. Perhaps I ought to begin by asking, 'What is a doctrine?' Let the reader be warned, then: nowhere in this book is there a definition of the word 'doctrine' such as might be found in a dictionary. Definitions of that kind have their value. They tell us how to use words properly, and the likes of Samuel Johnson and Noah Webster deserve our everlasting thanks for providing this information. But it was Johnson himself who defined a lexicographer as a harmless drudge, and prefaced his own dictionary with the comment that he was not so lost in lexicography as to forget that words are the children of earth and things the children of heaven. However important words may be—and they are extremely important—what they refer to is more important still. It is all too easy to suppose that you have understood what something is when you have learned its lexical definition, though all you have really understood is the way certain words fit together. The moral is this. The following chapters do aim at clarifying what doctrines are; more specifically, what Christian doctrines are. So this book is in some sense a kind of extended definition. But my hope is to aid the reader in arriving at more than the merely verbal understanding that computers, suitably programmed, can simulate. I will be defining doctrines not in words but by their relations to other things; not just verbally, that is, but functionally.

By way of illustrating the sort of definition I want to develop here, consider a chess set. Provided you know a bit about chess, you would have no trouble identifying which of the pieces are pawns. But suppose you were asked for a definition. What exactly *is* a pawn? You might start by describing visible features, but even a thorough and accurate description would not adequately answer the question. Chess sets come in all manner of designs, from plain to ornate and from conventional to futuristic, and consequently a description that fits the pawns in one set might well fit the kings or the bishops in another. The only way out of this quandary would be to abandon description altogether and take a different approach. Instead of scrutinizing individual pieces, you would have to turn your attention to what happens in an actual game. For what really makes each and every pawn a pawn is not its appearance but the way it functions, in relation to all the other pieces, within the activity of playing chess—how many squares it can move, in which direction, when, under what circumstances. That is why a pawn which reaches the opposite end of the board is no longer a pawn. It may look the same, but it is in fact a different piece, most likely a queen, because from then on it does everything a queen does. For similar reasons, a cork or a thimble used in place of a missing pawn *is* a pawn. It may look different from other pawns, but it fulfills the functional definition of pawnness.

Chess is only a game, of course. The movements that define its pieces are artificial. Much the same situation, however, would arise if you were asked to define what a kidney is. By itself, a kidney is an irregularly shaped organ with anatomical features that you might describe in detail. You might specify it more accurately by taking into account its position in the body, the paths of its ducts, and so forth. Finally, though, you would need a functional definition: an organ is a kidney if it plays a certain part, related in certain ways to certain other organs, in a certain set of biochemical processes. To define a kidney, in other words, is to understand what it does, not simply what it looks like or where it is located.

This leads to the key word in my title. In a well-known passage Aristotle proposes that "to understand the whatness of a thing is the same thing as to understand the *why* of it." His example is a lunar eclipse. What is it? Description is easy enough. An eclipse is a darkening of the moon. Very well; *why* then is the moon darkened in this way? Because the earth passes between the moon and the sun, blocking the sun's light and casting its own shadow on the moon. If you understand that, Aristotle says, you have understood an eclipse: the *why* of it explains what it is. Here again the thing to notice is that Aristotle is not content simply to paint a verbal picture. Describing an eclipse is only a first step towards what he wants to know. The 'whatness of a thing,' be it an eclipse or anything else, is not what it looks like or how it appears to an observer, but how it stands in relation to other things. In this case, the position of the earth in relation to the moon and the sun explains why an observable event, a lunar eclipse, appears as it does. And by specifying this set of relations, Aristotle goes beyond describing what an eclipse looks like, to defining what it is.

This book follows roughly the same procedure. It aims at understanding the *why* of doctrines by considering them in relation to other things. As the headings of the next five chapters indicate, each of them is about doctrines *and* something else—faith, community, authority, history, and scripture, in that order. The order is sequential in the sense that each chapter presupposes what has already been discussed, but that is only because a book has to start somewhere and then move in one direction. Each of the topics to be discussed, however, is so interwoven with all the others that I might have started with any of them, and in that sense chapters two through six are not links in a logical chain but avenues that converge on the same place from different angles.

The angles are different partly because 'Why doctrines?' is not so clear-cut a question as 'Why eclipses?' It can mean all sorts of things. 'Why doctrines?' can mean 'Why are there doctrines? How did they come to be?' Or, 'Why should there be doctrines? Why are they needed? What is the point of them?' Or again, 'Why do people, some people anyway, take doctrines seriously? How *can* they be taken seriously? Why not get rid of them?' These are questions of the broad and basic kind that will be explored here. I say explored, because my goal is not to arrive at neatly packaged answers. I hope rather to sketch a landscape and, perhaps, interest readers in pursuing a more thorough investigation on their own. Not that the landscape is stationary. It is constantly moving, like a game of chess. To use a better metaphor, doctrines are parts of an ecological system, a complicated, living, ongoing process, in which human thoughts and actions have a central role. Moreover, to explore this process is to participate in it. Answering the question 'Why doctrines?' is itself one of the activities that make doctrines what they are.

2

If my discussion is more detailed in some places than in others, it is because this book is partly the result of a personal quest. I have been asking 'Why doctrines?' for some time, and in none of the senses mentioned above has it been a rhetorical question. On one hand, it has always seemed to me that Christianity's stake in its doctrines is an important one. I can appreciate Dorothy L. Sayers's contention that

> it is a lie to say that dogma does not matter.... It is hopeless to offer Christianity as a vaguely idealistic aspiration of a simple and consoling kind; it is, on the contrary, a hard, tough, exacting and complex doctrine, steeped in a drastic and uncompromising realism.

Yet, on the other hand, there also seems to be something unattractive, even repugnant, about the very idea of dogma. John Henry Newman spoke of a 'dogmatic principle' in Christian religion, insisting that devotion without the fact of a supreme being is as meaningless as filial love without the fact of a parent. This principle, however, has never been self-evident, and it is far from being taken for granted today. In fact when Snoopy the beagle in the comic strip 'Peanuts' took it into his head to become a theologian, the ever-cynical Lucy was able to squelch his ambition with a pun. Snoopy, she pointed out, was too dogmatic. Many would say the same of Newman and Sayers.

There are good reasons for the bad taste dogma leaves in people's mouths. Its unsavory associations—arbitrariness, authoritarianism, intolerance, sectarian bigotry, superstition, patronizing smugness—can be justified with plenty of examples. Most of the arguments against dogmatism in this sense are familiar, and they need not be rehearsed here. This book is not, except by implication, a defense of doctrines in general or of the particular Christian doctrines it examines along the way. Objections and criticisms will, inevitably, be mentioned. But for the most part I will mention them only for the sake of sharpening some particular question that the reader will be left to chew on. As a friend who went through a draft of the book with a fine-tooth comb pointed out, the fact that I have not dotted every *i* or crossed every *t* raises all sorts of further questions, which set her thinking. That is exactly what I want to do. Questions come before answers, and if by the end of the book I have managed to make somewhat clearer just what is involved in the question 'Why doctrines?' I will have achieved my main objective.

This is not to say that I have tried to adopt a neutral viewpoint. For reasons I will lay out in due course, that is impossible. Another reader remarked that reading an early version of the following chapters was like spending an afternoon with their author. That too is as it should be. What I have written is not autobiography, and I hope it is not what Lucy would call too dogmatic. It does present a position, though, and where religion is concerned the stand that anyone takes is not in the long run separable from the person who takes it.

To put this another way, what you think about Christian doctrines depends in part on what you think about Christianity. I am not suggesting that raising and answering questions about doctrine is finally nothing more than working out the details of answers you have decided in advance. My point is simply that questions do not arise in a vacuum. If you are going to inquire why the moon is darkened, you need to have some preliminary notion of what an eclipse is. Likewise, a deliberate inquiry into the function of doctrines in Christianity needs some preliminary notion of 'the Christian thing,' some hunch as to where your inquiry is going, some acquaintance, which can only be personal, with what Christianity is all about. This background does not determine where your questions will lead you; it does provide the context for asking them at all.

The notion I will be elaborating on is summed up in the epigraph of this chapter. Religion, Christianity included, has two aspects, both essential. One of them, as Butler puts it in his *Analogy of Religion,* is "an inward principle, to be exerted in such and such inward acts of the mind and heart." Considered under this aspect, Christianity is essentially a matter of intimate, inner experience, a personal affair of feeling and affection; in fact, a love affair. Considered under its other aspect, which Butler calls outward or exterior, Christianity is public and social, characterized by forms of worship, traditions, organizational structures, symbols—and doctrines. This second aspect, then, will be my main concern. It is as essential, 'as real a part of religion, true religion,' as the first. But in order to understand why this is so, both aspects need to be considered together.

The spatial metaphor of interior and exterior is probably unavoidable. Unfortunately, it can be quite misleading. When it is taken as referring only to what is inside and outside a person's skin, there is a tendency to let the distinction fall apart and become a dichotomy, such that the essence of Christianity must be *either* inward and experiential *or* outward and doctrinal. And when that happens it is almost always the latter that gets short shrift. The outward aspect can come to be regarded as extrinsic and incidental, like the wrapper on a bar of chocolate. In that case, though it may be that some kind of outer husk is necessary, which kind it is will not much matter. Doctrines in particular will tend to be set over against experience and regarded as, at best, poetic descriptions of a religious dimension that is always present, though not always recognized, in our everyday awareness of ourselves. In the extreme, Christianity becomes the 'vaguely idealistic aspiration of a simple and consoling kind' that draws Sayers's fire in the quotation above.

That is one way of understanding how the inner and outer

aspects of Christianity are related. It is not the way followed in this book. My investigation of doctrines takes its bearings from a somewhat different view that can be stated this way.

Christianity is fundamentally a decision for a person: a decision that comes as a gift, for the person of Christ Jesus.

About this decision more will be said in the next chapter. It corresponds with Butler's 'inward principle, exerted in acts of the mind and heart.' It is immediate, in the sense of being interior and wholly personal. It is a decision, freely made, to live a certain way and become a certain sort of human being. But whereas other decisions are rooted in the kind of person you have already become, this decision uproots and transplants those who make it. *It* makes *them*. All their habits, predilections, and routines fall into a new pattern; all their actions take a new direction. They are enabled to be themselves, freed to act freely, given the ability to give. This freedom, however, would be merely formal, merely the absence of restraints, were it not for the specific meaning, content, and purpose that enter into the decision from outside. Christianity is founded on a decision. Equally, it is founded on what this decision is a decision for—not a general idea about the best way to live, but the meaning embodied and enacted in a particular human life.

To put it differently, Christian living is responding to a message. It is a personal answer to a personal, summoning word of address that consists neither in useful maxims nor in gnomic aphorisms but in a story. The outward aspect of Christianity is a vast and intricate set of variations on a narrative theme, and the center and summation of that theme is the story of what Jesus of Nazareth said and did and suffered.

Choosing this story is what conversion, in the specifically Christian sense, is all about. The choice itself is a gift. It happens. Living in accord with such a choice, however, involves working out what the Christian story means. For it is a message not only in the sense of a person-to-person address but also in the sense of a communication *about* something. And saying precisely what it is about is the whole point of Christian doctrines. They articulate Christianity's announcement, draw out its implications, state what it does and does not mean. Like the message itself, doctrines belong to the outer aspect of Christianity, and hence they are important in so far as the Christian story is intrinsically bound up with Christian conversion and the new life it generates.

This last sentence amounts to my own version of Newman's principle, and states in a very general way the thesis of this book. Devotion, prayer, worship, love, spirituality—these are beyond a doubt the heart and soul of Christian life. And all too often 'the letter killeth.' Yet neither of these is a reason for thinking that doctrines are superfluous. That they are, on the contrary, a treasure is the conviction I hope to share here.

The question 'Why doctrines?' does not arise in a vacuum but in a context that includes some provisional idea, more or less explicit and acknowledged, as to the sort of thing Christianity is. Even so, the question would be left vague and unfocused apart from some preliminary notion of what a doctrine is. I do not mean a definition; as I said at the outset, lexical definitions can easily short-circuit inquiry. Nor do I mean a least common denominator, gleaned from everything that could conceivably be called a doctrine. Instead, I mean an outstanding specimen, a standard or typical example or central case. Here, I have two such examples in mind. Although they do not appear until halfway through the book, they are never far in the background and it is appropriate to mention them now.

The doctrines I have adopted as focal instances are those of the Incarnation and the Trinity, more especially as they are set out in that "great humanist Ode" which is usually referred to as the Athanasian Creed. Why I have chosen these particular doctrines as exemplars can be summed up under three heads. First, because they are the very core of Christianity. All its other

precepts and tenets are anchored here. Second, because they are
sometimes thought to be arcane and incomprehensible—a judgment that may turn out upon examination to be exaggerated.
Third, because they are held in common by nearly all groups,
denominations, and confessions that go by the name of Christian.

My three reasons are closely intertwined. The first two will
become clearer in the following chapters, but about the third
something needs to be said here. I have already pointed out that
when it comes to understanding religion there are no neutral
corners. Everyone takes a stand. As the selection of authors
quoted at the beginning of each chapter indicates, mine is a position shaped by one of many currents in the stream of Christianity. How deeply this confessional tradition has influenced my
book will probably be more evident to some of those who read
it than to me. Nevertheless I have tried to pose my question
about doctrines in a way that will be relevant to a wider audience.
Doctrine is one thing that divides Christians along confessional
lines, but their disagreements on this score are less momentous
than the great doctrines they hold in common. Moreover, the
deepest division has almost nothing to do with denominational
boundaries; it is not about any particular doctrine but about
whether doctrines as such mean anything at all. And that is
exactly the kind of question I hope to explore.

❦ TWO ❦
Doctrines and Faith

For as love is the God that created all things, so love is the purity, the perfection, and blessing of all created things; and nothing can live in God but as it lives in love.

WILLIAM LAW

I N SIX SIMPLE words, now famous, John Wesley recounts what happened to him on 24 May 1783: "I felt my heart strangely warmed." That he is describing a 'religious' experience can easily be gathered from the circumstances in which it occurred. Meetings like the one in London's Aldersgate Street that he was attending that night, books such as the one that was being read aloud as he listened, language of the kind he used in his journal to record the whole episode—all of these fall under the rubric of religion as the word is ordinarily used. No doubt they all had their influence on what occurred. Yet none of them, I want to suggest, was essential. The external setting did not determine the strange warming of Wesley's heart, and classifying his experience on the basis of its setting alone runs the risk of putting things the wrong way round. Neither the antecedents of religious experience nor its consequences make it religious: what happens *between* 'before' and 'after' is what lies at the core of religion. Books and meetings, ceremonies, buildings, and institutions, ways of thinking and feeling and behaving are 'religious' in so far as they are connected in some way with a change, a warming of the heart that is strange precisely because it is out of all proportion to anything and everything that surrounds it.

I hope to make the meaning of this sentence clearer presently by means of a few examples. First, there are two general

comments that need to be made. One is that I do not for a
moment suppose that experience, religious or other, comes 'neat.'
Pure experience is like pure water: it may exist, but samples of
it are extremely rare. By and large our experience is interpreted
experience, experience that takes place within a conscious flow of
words and memories and images. We experience the new in relation to what is at least to some extent familiar already. Even the
most imaginative writer of science fiction can describe what it
would be to experience a wholly new world—say, on another
planet—only by describing what it is *like*, by weaving together
terrestrial sights and sounds and so forth.

Yet I do not for a moment suppose that our experience is
simply determined by what we can already talk about. That is my
second general comment. Language is not a set of cookie cutters
that impose their own pattern, more or less mechanically, on
shapeless experiential dough. Coming to understand what is
given in experience is a far more subtle process than that. To
state as succinctly as possible the point that bears on this chapter
and the next one, noticing what we have no words for is unlikely
but not impossible. Our presuppositions and habitual ways of
thinking about previous experiences do not dictate what we can
be attentive to in the present. They do influence it. To a great
extent we see what we are prepared to see, and overlook what
we are not.

My reason for introducing this pair of comments at the outset
is this. To pigeonhole, under the label 'religious,' the kind of
experience Wesley describes can all too easily lead to its being
overlooked or disregarded. People for whom that word conjures
up stained glass and organ music are often inclined to say that
no such thing has ever happened to *them*, thank you. And much
that has been written about religious experience from a scholarly
standpoint tends to stress its uncanniness. Either way, the holy
or the sacred can be conceived as a realm so far removed from the
everyday world as to suggest not only that the experience itself
is strange and special—which it is—but also that it is utterly

different from anything that ordinary people ordinarily encounter—which it is not. They may not notice it. They may
dismiss it as unimportant or freakish. They may, and often do,
describe it in words drawn from some vocabulary that is not
explicitly religious, a psychological one for example.

Yet it happens, and what it is that happens can best be conveyed by a series of examples, some of them personal but none
of them, I hope, esoteric. Each is intended to give the reader an
opportunity to recall some similar occasion, some personal
experience, that my description more or less fits. Further, the
examples are cumulative. They lead up to religious experience,
but that is not where they set out from. I begin instead, pro-
saically enough, with learning to ride a bicycle.

2

Acquiring the knack of propelling oneself on two wheels
is a kind of watershed, a small one perhaps, but for a youngster
often momentous. I expect that is why I remember so vividly
how it happened to me. Clutching the handlebars for dear life,
I looked over my shoulder and saw my grandmother, twenty
feet behind, waving. For the better part of an hour this
redoubtable lady had trotted alongside the bicycle I was pedal-
ling, helping me keep my balance as I picked up speed, pushing
me along, letting go—whereupon I had consistently toppled
over. This time, however, it had worked. My riding was a bit
wobbly, true, but I was wobbling by myself. What had been
insuperably difficult up to that moment was now, by comparison,
happening effortlessly.

What had changed? The bicycle, in itself, was the same. I was
different. And therefore the relationship between me and bicycles
was also different. Having been only a potential bicycler, someone
with the requisite limbs and muscles, I was an actual bicycler, and
bicycles, which as far as I was concerned had been only a potential

means of transportation, were now actual vehicles. There was
nothing inevitable about the change. It depended on all sorts of
things, notably an energetic grandmother, yet when it occurred
the result was not simply a continuation of what had preceded it.
There was something new. A capacity I was born with had become
an ability in practice, a skill, or (using the word in its strict sense)
a habit.

The kind of transition I have just described is fairly commonplace. Swimming, ice skating, or any number of similar skills
might be substituted for it. My second illustration may be less
familiar, for it has to do with conversation, and genuine conversation, as contrasted with passing the time, exchanging information, small talk, and in general speaking *at* other people, is rarer
than we commonly suppose. I have in mind what happened when
I and a colleague of mine, members of an informal committee,
arrived one morning at the usual meeting room only to learn that
the third member of our caucus would be delayed. As we waited
we began to chat. Not surprisingly, since we already knew each
other and had professional interests in common, we were soon
happily talking shop. The transition to another, quite different
level of communication would be difficult to reproduce in
dialogue, but it happened. Talk that began as a serious but
pleasant confabulation quietly turned a corner. It took on a new
dimension of personal sympathy, good will, harmony. Two
human beings, already friendly in the conventional sense, started
to be friends; above and beyond our shared understanding of what
we were talking about, we began to understand each other.

Here again it is the change that I want to underscore. It was
neither stunning nor dramatic. Things went on afterwards pretty
much as they had before. They went on, however, with a new
energy and a richer meaning, because the feelings that animated
a personal relationship had been transformed. Two people were
different. Yet it was no mere spurt of emotion that changed
them. It was a gift that was not, and could not have been, manu-
factured or compelled; as Louis Armstrong said of jazz, 'If you
gotta ask what it is you'll never know.'

This leads to my third example, which an anecdote will introduce. A certain barber is said to have told the novelist and literary critic Charles Williams, while cutting his hair, "When my girl's about, I'm that happy I don't feel as if I had an enemy in the world. I'd forgive anybody anything." At this Williams jumped from the chair, wrung the barber's hand, and cried, "My dear man, that's exactly what Dante said!"

What he said took the shape of a poem, perhaps the greatest poem in European literature, *The Divine Comedy*. Dante was moved to write it by an experience that brought into focus the explanation and goal of everything, the *why* of the world. In and through another person, Beatrice, he met what every person ought to be, and became a different person himself. "The quality of love which springs from Beatrice and beholds Beatrice seems to 'drive far off each thing of sin and guilt,' " Williams writes in his study of Dante's poetry. "Dante has to become the thing he has seen in Beatrice, and has, for that moment, seen in himself." He could forgive anybody anything. Yet the only exceptional thing about his vision is that he took it so seriously. The whole dramatic panorama of *The Divine Comedy* from hell to heaven is neither more nor less than an incomparably beautiful elaboration of what happened to Williams's barber.

It can happen to anyone. What Williams calls the Beatrician moment has recently begun to be acknowledged by psychologists, especially those whose attention has shifted from pathology and sickness to wholeness and health. Abraham Maslow, to take a frequently cited example, makes a strong case for revising the established view of psychic well-being as being well adjusted; as stability, that is, or equilibrium. Human living, on that view, is like a mattress: you pound out as many lumps as you can and cope with the rest. Maslow, by contrast, argues that being human is not, at its best, a kind of steady state, a possession that needs only to be fine-tuned, but a process. The problem of living is not how to anesthetize desires and longings; it is how to sort them out. For, in healthy people, the tension they produce is not so much an annoyance or a neuralgia, an itch that demands to be scratched, as a motivation for growth. "Capacities clamor to be used," Maslow writes, "and cease their clamor only when they *are* well used." Like the capacity of bicycle-riding and the capacity of friendship, the capacity to *be*, to become the kind of person you truly are, has to be made real in practice.

No more than one adult in a hundred, according to Maslow, is what he would call a self-actualizer, someone who never stops growing. But he also suggests that many of the other ninety-nine percent, and perhaps all, know what it is to become themselves by surpassing themselves. That is what happens in the ecstatic or 'peak' experiences discussed in Maslow's most widely known books: people live for a time as they were meant to live. Mystical, oceanic, transcendent—call the experience what you will, it transforms those to whom it happens. And because they are different, so is everything in relation to them. As they are more alive, so the world they are alive to is complete, whole, 'just as it should be'; a world to be cherished, contemplated, and relished rather than used or manipulated. As Maslow puts it, the individual and his or her world "become more like each other as both move towards perfection."

Whether all peak experiences are the same as Dante's Beatrician moment is not a question that has to be settled here. But it is interesting to note the similarity of Maslow's descriptions to an account of religious experience which, fictional though it is, comes from the pen of one who knew at first hand what he was writing about. C.S. Lewis portrays what happened to one of the characters in his novel *That Hideous Strength* as follows. Jane Studdock is walking in a garden, thinking of other things, when, "at one particular corner of the gooseberry patch, the change came." Not a visible change. The ground and the moss were the same. Nevertheless a boundary had been passed. "There was nothing, and never had been anything, like this. Yet also, everything had been like this; only by being like this had anything existed." What Jane thought of as herself, as *me*, vanished. *Me* became the name of someone who did not yet exist, but whose existence was called for, inexorably, in a demand that was "the origin of all right demands and contained them." She knew herself as a person, but at the same time as something, something made, "a thing being made at this very moment, without its choice, in a shape it had never dreamed of. And the making went on amidst a kind of splendour or sorrow or both, whereof she could not tell whether it was in the moulding hands or in the kneaded lump."

Words, Lewis continues, take too long. The largest thing that had ever happened to Jane Studdock had occurred in a moment, and as it became a memory its place was taken by the howl and chatter of voices that "have not joy." Jane's first reaction was suspicious caution. "Take care. Draw back. Keep your head. Don't commit yourself." Then came an urge to use her experience as an instrument. "How much better you will now understand the Seventeenth-Century poets!" Finally, the voice of control. "Go on. Try to get it again."

Religious experience is susceptible of all these distortions, and others besides. It can be indulged in; worse, it can be counterfeited. Bishop Butler's chilly response to Wesley's enthusiasm is, in the strictest sense, true: 'Sir, the pretending to extraordinary revelations and gifts . . . is a horrid thing, a very horrid thing.' But excesses and imitations, here as elsewhere, depend for their existence on the genuine article. If there were no real diamonds nobody would bother to fake them. Conversely, those who have felt their own hearts strangely warmed can recognize what words will never convey, and it is they who have to discriminate between the gold and the sand.

3

What is religious experience like? It is like waking up, like entering a real and compassionate conversation, like turning a corner and seeing for the first time that 'only by being like this had anything existed.' It is like acquiring a habit or skill: what used to be difficult becomes easy, except that instead of bringing about a new relationship with one thing or one person, the change affects everything and everyone. The ability one acquires is the 'habit of being'—not just the being of a biological organism or a bundle of emotions and reflexes, but that being which is a becoming, a self-surpassing, a being *for*. 'Give me a person in love,' said Augustine. 'He knows what I mean.' Cheapened and sentimentalized though the word has been, there is no other. Religious experience is being in love.

What goes by the name of love is often only the gratification of a need, a return to equilibrium. The effect of this kind of love is not unlike the relief aspirin brings to a headache. But there is also a love that transforms, releases new energy, frees those who experience it by pulling them out of their self-enclosed desires and fears and launching them in a new direction. Such was the love that Dante encountered. It is easy to say he wrote his poem in order to compensate for having lost Beatrice—too easy, because it lets us feel superior to him. We may not write so well as he did, that is, but neither will we be taken in by what he wrote. Nor will we understand it, though, unless we take him at his word. *The Divine Comedy* is less a fantasy, spun to replace love lost, than an attempt to express what Dante had begun to find, and an extension of that discovery. Beatrice herself was the occasion of Dante's love, and therefore the *Comedy* portrays her as the guide and the way to abundant life. Yet in the poem as in the experience that inspired it, she is incidental—an image, as Williams puts it, of something that cannot in itself be imagined. Dante was truly in love with Beatrice, but he was even more truly in love through Beatrice. The content of his experience far outpassed its occasion.

Without some image, there could be no grasp of what religious experience means, for it is through images that we come to understand everything we experience. But while religious experience is always associated with particular occasions, at least to begin with, it is not tied to any particular *kind* of occasion. In the arts, what is appropriately though vaguely referred to as romanticism is often the result of an experience of nature as the image or sensible vision of insensible glory. The love of human lovers, however, has always been a privileged metaphor for religious experience, partly because it is personal. If Williams's barber could forgive anybody anything, it was because his love made it easy for him to do what would otherwise have been the hardest thing in the world, namely, give up a grudge. And it was easy because he could see beyond the behavior of others and recognize them as valuable in themselves. Paradoxically, it is personal involvement, intimacy, conversation in the sense used earlier, that makes unclouded vision and objective judgment possible.

"So impressive is this," to quote Maslow, "that, far from accepting the common platitude that love makes people blind, I become more and more inclined to think of the *opposite* as true, namely that non-love makes us blind." Being in love enables us to discern values in ourselves, in others, in our world. Instead of construing things and people as means to some end and treating them accordingly—which is what most of us do, much of the time—we can regard them for their own sake, simply as what they are and what they were therefore meant to be.

"You talk as if life were good." So says a character in *Descent into Hell*, one of the best and eeriest of Charles Williams's novels. In the reply to this remark Williams states his own view: "It's either good or evil, and you can't decide that by counting events on your fingers. The decision is of another kind." It is of another kind because it determines the ground on which all other, more particular assessments and evaluations are built. Whether the very word 'good' means something more than convenient, pleasant, satisfying, or expedient depends on this kind of decision; so does confidence in the worthwhileness of living, or basic trust that finally the universe is friendly, or conviction as to the intrinsic goodness of things. No one can be argued into an assurance

so fundamental as this, or argued out of it. Like the love in which
it is rooted, a decision of the sort that Williams is referring to is a
gift. To some it is given in installments, through many channels,
beginning from childhood with affectionate trust in their parents
and widening to encompass the whole of life. Others receive it
later and all at once. But however it comes it is a permanent
revolution that changes 'whatever is, is good' from a mere and
facile slogan into the steadfast affirmation of a lover, one whose
acceptance of the world and of self comes of having been
accepted.

Not that cruelty, oppression, and suffering are invisible to the
'eyes of love.' Far from it. It is the saints who are most acutely
aware of wickedness, first of all in themselves. As Austin Farrer
has put it, good and evil are qualities "revealed to us by the
motion of our heart. Evil is what, after all consideration, it
detests, and good, what it embraces." And this motion is strongest
in both directions when it is the pulse of a heart strangely
warmed. To embrace life as good and the universe as friendly is
at the same time to know that evil is a betrayal, a failure of
goodness, a lack of love as darkness is a lack of light. In other
words, to detest any action or situation, any policy or institution
or system, is to be aware that it ought to be better. But what is
the origin of 'ought' and 'better' if not an implicit comparison
with right action, wholesome situation, benevolent policy,
valuable institution, worthwhile system? That such comparisons
can be drawn, that 'ought' rests on more than arbitrary whim and
'better' on more than momentary fancy, is the sum and substance
of the basic attitude I am discussing here. Apart from such a
stance, neither outrage at the world's ills nor efforts to overcome
them would have any meaning. Human life itself would lack all
significance. One action would be as absurd as the next. And that
way madness lies.

The alternative is to take evil seriously. But it is not the last
word, because it is not the first. Evil is a lie, a false fact, a distortion of what is essentially and in itself good. *Why* our world

should be infested with "the fearsome, word-and-thought-defy-
ing banality of evil" is a problem that puts notorious difficulties
in the way of affirming that whatever is, is good. Yet Hannah
Arendt's phrase is accurate. The problem of evil defies our
words and our thoughts. The difficulties it presents are intellectual difficulties, and ten thousand such difficulties, John Henry
Newman observed, do not make a doubt. Evil would not be a
problem were it not for the kind of basic trust that begins from
Pascal's 'reasons of the heart' and goes on to inform actions,
thoughts, and words.

To sum up the present section, love is a state of mind as well
as of feeling. A change of heart brings about change in the stand
one takes on the most fundamental issues of human existence,
and the gift of a love without limits or conditions give rise to
convictions that I propose from here on to call 'faith,' as dis-
tinguished from 'belief.' These two words have been used in too
many ways, and too much has been written about them, for any
definition to satisfy everyone. The most I can hope for is to
adopt a usage that is reasonably clear and not unreasonably
arcane. 'Faith,' then, pertains here to the orientation of a person's
whole being; 'belief,' to what men and women hold to be true.
Faith is an all-pervading conviction that underlies every decision
and every action, irrespective of whether one is aware of it;
belief is a more or less explicit act of the mind, directed towards
verbal expressions. Faith depends on who you are; belief, on
what has been proposed to you for acceptance or rejection,
assent or dissent. This distinction is not a disjunction. There is
nevertheless a difference, which needs to be set out as clearly as
possible before the relationship between faith and belief is
discussed.

4

First, faith. Wilfred Cantwell Smith, highly regarded for his
work in comparative and historical studies of religion, gives a fine
delineation.

Faith is a quality of human living, which at its best has taken the form of serenity and courage and service; a quiet confidence and joy that enable one to feel at home in the universe, and to find meaning in the world and in one's life, a meaning that is profound and ultimate, and stable no matter what may happen to oneself at the level of immediate event. Men and women of this kind of faith face catastrophe or confusion, affluence or sorrow, unperturbed, face opportunity with conviction and drive, and face others with self-forgetting charity.

Having faith is being certain that there is something to live for, some purpose or direction or goal, a reason why life goes on and should go on. There are, of course, many things to live for, such as family, nation, job, other people's esteem, justice, pleasure, knowledge, or property. Any of these can be what Paul Tillich calls an ultimate concern, and in that sense become the object of faith. In the religious sense, however, faith is something more. It is knowledge that depends on conversion, knowledge apprehended in the light of love, knowledge that is conscious yet not the self-generated product of conscious reasoning. It is the knowledge not only that life is worth living but also that it is *made to be* worth living. Hence, in H.R. Niebuhr's words, "to have faith and to have a god is one and the same thing."

Why? In the first place, to be in love is always to be in love with someone. In the second, love without restrictions or qualifications can only be the love of someone who is similarly unrestricted. In the third, to know as a result of such a love that life is meaningful and the world is good is to know and rely on this transcendent someone as the bestower of significance and worth. And these three implications of religious conversion, taken together, yield a rough but recognizable definition of deity. 'A transcendent, personal source of being and value'—that, to borrow Thomas Aquinas's famous line, is what everyone means by God.

I am not suggesting that religious experience establishes that there is in fact a God. That is a further question. I am suggesting only that conversion, being turned towards a mysterious Other, is what gives the name 'God' its primary meaning. Faith and deity are correlatives. God is defined in the first instance as one partner in a relationship, the person with whom a religiously converted man or woman is in love. All further definitions— 'maker of heaven and earth,' 'ground of being,' 'First Cause'— are extensions, derivatives, or corollaries. What the word 'God' means, to put it another way, depends on who is using it. Everyone knows its nominal meaning as an item in the vocabulary common to all English-speakers, but in the prayer of a religious person it has a significance quite different from the one it has in a flippant oath. Genuinely religious people know what they are talking about, though often they prefer not to talk at all. And the fact that there are no linguistic or cultural bounds on the experience that gives them this knowledge is what grounds the distinction I have drawn between faith and belief. Cantwell Smith sums it up in an aphorism: "One's faith is given by God, one's beliefs by one's century." Words and concepts, that is, evolve. They depend on historical circumstances. Faith does not.

Yet this is not to say that words and concepts, the symbols that give faith an articulate shape, have no importance. It matters enormously whether you think of faith in terms of the Idea of Freedom or Progress or Nature or simply The Beyond. If instead you choose to speak of God, it will be because you have discerned something appropriate in the way other people use the word. Notice that I have said *choose*. Expressing your faith in some way is not optional, but how you express it is. The decision need not be deliberate and open-eyed; the expressions you use can simply be 'given by your century' and accepted more or less unreflectively. Be that as it may, you will at some level have made a choice: what others have said, you too will say. You might, for example, interpret religious experience, the strange warming of the heart, as the gift of the Holy Spirit or the grace of God or both. If so, you are in a literal sense taking someone else's word for it, and your decision to adopt that word as your own is a decision to believe.

That is how believing will be understood here, as 'taking someone else's word for it.' So defined, believing in the specifically religious sense is a special case of something that pervades every corner of life. Human knowledge is a common fund; believing spreads the wealth. Very few of us ever contribute something that has never been known before, but all of us draw on it continually. Unless you happened to hear the Gettysburg Address as it was being delivered, you know what Lincoln said (if you do know it) because you found it in a book. Unless you have spent a long time experimenting with flour and water and yeast, you know how to bake bread (if you do know it) because you first followed a recipe or because someone showed you how, which amounts to the same thing. Unless you have explored all the streets in Cleveland, you know your way around town (if you do know it) because you have consulted a map. And so on.

These examples may be trivial, but what they illustrate is a division of labor in which all of us participate from the time we learn our native language, and which is as much a part of highly erudite knowledge as of commonplace know-how. Scientists, for instance, have quite enough to do simply to keep abreast of current developments in their own fields, without going back and repeating the whole succession of observations, hypotheses, and experiments carried out by their predecessors in those fields. Scientific knowledge is shared. It depends on collaboration and therefore, to the same extent, science depends on belief. So does every other field of human endeavor, from politics to poker to Persian history.

To believe is to accept the truth of some statement, to say in effect, 'Yes, that is so.' But in fact this is only the final step in a three-step process. As 'taking someone else's word for it,' believing is always believing someone as well as something. 'Yes, that is so' depends on 'Yes, so-and-so is reliable, competent, knowledgeable, expert; in short, so-and-so is to be believed.' This, however, depends in turn on a still more basic judgment. Usually tacit, it amounts to 'Yes, believing is in general a good thing; dividing the labor and sharing the wealth promote the human enterprise of knowing.' In sum, we assent to any particular proposition not simply because it is believable in itself but because we have confidence in the person who proposes it and also because we approve of collaboration where knowledge is concerned.

For example, suppose I say that I know my car is starting badly because the spark plugs are worn out. The bad starting I am familiar with from experience, but the condition of the spark plugs I accept (being thoroughly ignorant of such things) on the say-so of the mechanic at the garage. And I accept it for two reasons. First, in my judgment the mechanic knows his business; second, in my judgment it is a good thing that there are people who specialize in spark plugs. The situation might, however, be more complicated. My reliance on the mechanic's expertise might itself be second-hand, if for example, the garage was recommended by a friend whom I judge to have had enough experience with the garage in question to know whether its staff is reliable. In that case, my more general judgment would be that for the most part it is wise to take the recommendations of the experienced, especially when they are friends and as such not prone to deliberate mendacity.

A decision to believe is thus a complex act of choosing. By and large the complexity goes unnoticed, but the three-stage structure I have just outlined is always at work. I have discussed it at some length partly because it helps to elucidate the ambiguous phrase 'belief in.' To start with the easiest case, statements such as 'I believe in evolution' or 'I believe in the Loch Ness monster' present no particular difficulty. Each is an instance of my accepting that something is so—the first, that a certain process has occurred; the second, that the wildlife of Scotland includes an exceptionally large and camera-shy reptile. Each in turn rests on an instance of my confidence in someone—in the majority of biologists on one hand, in a few eyewitnesses and whoever it was that took the famous snapshot of Nessie on the other. And ultimately both rest on my approval of the division of labor whereby some people specialize in a particular branch of natural science and others in monster-watching, neither of which I have the time or inclination to pursue for myself.

These two examples are straightforward, however, because they represent a fairly modern way of using 'believe.' It was once virtually the same as 'belove,' and this older meaning endures in statements like 'I believe in Judith.' Here the implication is not that I am sure Judith exists, but that I have no qualms in relying on her honesty, integrity, guilelessness, and similar qualities. In fact, 'I believe in Judith' verges on meaning that I have faith in her, that I trust her, that I am and will remain loyal to her. In terms of my three-stage analysis, 'I believe in Judith' combines believing something (namely that Judith is a certain kind of person) with believing someone (namely Judith herself). What I accept as true *about* her can scarcely be separated from my confidence *in* her as the source of what I accept.

What then of 'I believe in God'? I have already suggested that the meaning of 'God' depends on the kind of person using it. For some people 'I believe in God' says far more than 'God exists.' It is not a remark about their position, but the very act by which they adopt it. To say 'I believe in God' with all seriousness is to commit myself, come what may, to a policy or style of living. Thus the meaning of what I say is the substance of my commitment, and that meaning lies somewhere in the future. 'I believe in God' is less a statement than a promise. At the same time, living out a commitment depends partly on knowing to whom I am committed. Having faith is the same as having a God, but no one has simply *a* God. It is always *this* God, a God about whom certain statements are made. Faith may be given by God, but that it is *God* who gives it is a belief.·

Not that the distinction is easy to make in practice. There is such a thing as crypto-theism, a kind of vague and unreflective confidence in 'a power not ourselves that makes for goodness,' and where the line should be drawn between this on one hand

and belief in God on the other is a question that does not admit of general answers. Moreover, the strange warming of the heart, as experienced, does not in itself disclose the identity of its source. 'Who am I in love with?' is a further question. At the same time, however, it was pointed out earlier in this chapter that what we experience we almost invariably experience *as* this, that, or the other. Consequently, how I answer the question 'Who am I in love with?'—what I choose to believe, that is, about the origin and implications of religious experience—is never totally independent of what I already think and know and believe about other things.

It is here that all the tough questions about religious belief arise. Analyzing the formal structure of deciding to believe is one thing; justifying, explaining, or defending the decision to believe in God is something else, something far more difficult. There are strong arguments against the kind of assertion believers make, among which the classical one has been mentioned already. The problem of evil, as an objection to belief in God, runs like this:

> God is the absolute case of a personal agent?—Yes.—That means He is omnipotent and good?—Yes.—Does omnipotent goodness have practical consequences?—Yes.—Will a good person who has the power prevent harm from befalling the innocent?—Yes.—Then will not almighty goodness prevent all harm from happening to all the innocent?—Mm.—Is there a single verifiable generalization about visible misfortunes which God will, or will not, permit to befall any definable class of people?

There have been hundreds of variations on this theme. Simplistic or sophisticated, they appear to have logic on their side. But for exactly that reason, what I suggested earlier still holds: such arguments raise difficulties, not doubts. Job would not have been outraged at the catastrophes that beset him, had he not been sure that they were somehow unjust; nor would he have railed at God for allowing them to occur, had he not been sure that God is the wellspring of justice. What Job believes about the justness of God at the end of the tale is different, but that is because from first to last he believes that God is, somehow, just.

In any case, the problem of reconciling the infinite love that changes human hearts with the woes that wrench them apart is not always the biggest obstacle to belief in God. Modern atheism does not appeal directly to philosophical logic. The soil it is rooted in is a compost of conceptions and assessments of the human situation all of which, in different ways, stress humanity's coming of age as both a fact and an imperative. We have to seize control of our destiny in this world, claim the freedom and autonomy that is ours by right, live the austere yet heroic life of those who make their own way. Whatever impedes the progress of this conquest of ourselves and our environment, by tying us to childish ways, is intolerable and must be swept away. Above all, God has got to go. Indeed, did we but know it, he is gone. For, it is claimed, belief in God is nothing but a diversion, a detour away from the true path towards human well-being. Or it is nothing but the people's opium, a drug with which they dose themselves to avoid the pain of self-sovereignty. Or it is nothing but a collective neurosis, a displacement of feeling onto an illusory father-figure, by which we postpone the harsh reality of growing up. Or, finally, it is nothing but the source and product of a servile cowardice that denies life, stifles creativity, and degrades all that is most noble.

Voltaire, Marx, Freud, Nietzsche. These are the names associated, respectively, with the critiques just summarized. But their names do not matter; the case they argued for has become common property. Their objections suffuse an atmosphere that we cannot help breathing and, for some, count decisively against the credibility of God. Certainly none of those objections is to be taken lightly. They are all, so far as they go, correct. Religious belief can be a diversion, a surrogate, and all the rest. In many cases it is. The important question, though, is whether it can also be, and in many cases is, something else. Is the fulfillment of human self-creation to be found in power, or rather in love? Is that abundant life a prize to be captured by heroic struggles, or rather a gift? Does liberation in its truest sense consist in autonomy, the absence of restraints, or rather in personal commitment to one 'whose service is perfect freedom'?

None of these is a question that can be answered by counting events on your fingers. The decision is of another kind, and has to be made over and over. It was Jean-Paul Sartre who said that atheism is a long-range affair. So is belief. Religious conversion is its foundation; there is no other; yet conversion is the beginning of a lifelong conversation. God speaks the first word, silently. But religious love is like other loves in that it calls for a response, an answering gesture expressed in words as well as in deeds. That is the meaning of worship. Those who pray do not address a nameless, unidentified Thou. Prayer is a declaration of commitment, a pledge of allegiance, but also an assertion of what God has done and is doing for those who love him.

O God, from whom all holy desires, all good counsels, and all just works do proceed....

Blessed art thou, O Lord our God, King of the universe, who createst the fruit of the vine....

My soul doth magnify the Lord,
and my spirit hath rejoiced in God my Savior...
He hath put down the mighty from their seat,
and hath exalted the humble and meek....

Our Father, who art in heaven....

There are other ways of characterizing God, and those who use them in responding to an inner gift of love would be the last to say that any form of words is adequate. Yet wordless prayer, the mystics' cloud of unknowing, is rather the ideal of worship than its starting point. Prayer ordinarily includes ascriptions and affirmations that are—though they are far more than—statements of belief.

The fact that people still worship does not in itself refute the modern claim that God is dead. But since worship is the primary home of religious language in general and assertions of belief in particular, those who know what it is to pray are in a better position to discriminate between genuine belief and self-delusion than those who are merely spectators. Discernment of spirits is not like sorting tomatoes, because sanctity is not a perceptible quality like size and color. You recognize it in so far as you have been given it. And recognizing sanctity in others is the most compelling reason to take their word for who it is that sanctifies. Belief in God, like other kinds of belief, is a collaborative venture.

The next chapter will have more to say on that. Here, the point I am concerned to make is that beliefs are intrinsic to religion. If they were not, there would be no need to defend or explain them. This is not, however, to suggest that religion can be defined as a more or less coherent set of beliefs: that would be like saying that a skeleton *per se* is a ballet dancer. I use the comparison advisedly. Jellyfish, being boneless, do not dance. Neither, on its own, does a skeleton. That animated sculpture which is ballet is a coordinated involvement of the whole body, and that way of living towards transcendence which is religion involves the whole person—heart, soul, mind, and strength. Beliefs are not the most important part of this orientation of life, but neither are they incidental to it. Religious conversion kindles a fire that gives light as well as heat; it does change the mind, because it changes the heart. To be in love with someone without wanting to know more about that person would be something less than human. But the person to whom one is related in religious love has been loved before. Believing, in the religious sense, is learning from others what they have found out about the love of God.

5

This leads, at long last, to doctrines. A doctrine is something learned, because, as the word implies, it is something taught. In this general sense doctrine refers to any explicit position, taken on some important question, formulated in words, and proposed for others to accept as what is or ought to be true. Doctrines are statements to the effect that such-and-such is the case with regard to this or that state of affairs. Thus the doctrine of states' rights and the doctrine of separation of powers are assertions about how the United States is to be constituted as a nation, the Monroe doctrine is an assertion about America's position with respect to other nations, and all three have implications for what ought to be so in specific aspects of national policy. Similarly there are economic doctrines, capitalism and socialism being the principal ones at present, each with its variations and subdivisions. There are doctrines about how human action is motivated, such as behaviorism, and doctrines about how it should be motivated, such as utilitarianism; doctrines about the composition of the universe and the composition of a poem, doctrines about the nature of life, human destiny, and so on. In ethics, philosophy, psychology, jurisprudence, and every other field that raises questions to which the answers are not obvious, each of the positions that have been adopted has also been expressed formally as doctrine.

There is no need here to distill from these examples a definition that would serve to distinguish doctrines from theories, decrees, precepts, and other general teachings. I am more concerned with the place of doctrines in religion, specifically their relation to religious experience, faith, and belief. That the last of these bears most directly on doctrines may already be clear. For if a doctrine is a statement which proposes that something is so, it follows that to subscribe to a doctrine is not simply to learn it and grasp what it proposes, but also to accept the truth of the proposal, to say in effect, 'Yes, that is so'; in a word, to believe it. Such an assent is a matter of decision, although often enough the decision is made tacitly and without explicit deliberation, and the decision that issues in 'Yes, that is so' is in fact the last of three steps, although often enough the other two go unnoticed. All of this applies to believing the doctrines of a religion. Faith, not belief, is the human counterpart of deity, but I have suggested that nobody has faith in an unspecified X. Having faith is equivalent to having a God, but everyone believes something *about* his or her God; for example, "that he exists and that he rewards those who seek him" (Heb 11:6).

Both of these statements are doctrines in the sense I have just explained. Both are fairly broad, and what they propose is not especially abstruse or controversial—or so it would seem to most if not all religious people. But this last clause is in fact saying a great deal. That God exists is not self-evident in the way it is self-evident that triangles have three sides. The three-sidedness of a triangle cannot be denied consistently; the existence of God can be, and for reasons mentioned in the previous section, it is. As for his rewarding those who seek him, think of Job. Nevertheless there are people who do believe these and other doctrines, people who have decided, 'Yes, that is so.' Why?

Deciding to believe any religious doctrine comes about through the same threefold process that constitutes other acts of believing. It involves trusting someone, namely the person or persons who profess the doctrine in question, as well as approving of belief in general. But it involves more. Religious doctrines make sense only to the eye of faith. Not that the decision to believe them simply bypasses the arguments *pro* and *con*. The point is rather that argument, by itself, cannot and does not tip the scales. The credibility of doctrines rests on discernment as well as intelligence. Only love is believable, and those who approve of a division of labor where religious truth is concerned, and trust whoever it was that brought particular doctrines to their attention, do it for the love of God. For it is that unmerited and unconditional love which generates the convictions of faith, and it is in light of faith that one can discern the evidence, the warrants, the reasons that count decisively in choosing to believe the particular teachings of a particular religion.

This last sentence is the gist of the present chapter. It locates doctrines in the context of religious conversion by setting faith prior to belief and love prior to both. That, I would contend, is the personal or 'existential' order of priorities. It helps if a convincing case can be mounted for the cogency and value of some doctrinal assertion; it helps far more if the assertion in question is not only taught but also acted on by people whose living is the embodiment of holiness; yet when all is said *and* done the decision to believe is personal. It springs from a heart strangely warmed.

This is not to say that the priority of religious experience to acceptance of doctrine is necessarily, or even usually, the chronological order of events. Wesley might have responded to his Aldersgate experience by asking himself whether it meant that he was going crazy. That happens. Maslow cites the case of a convinced Marxist who finally and with great difficulty succeeded in persuading herself that a 'peak' experience, which she knew perfectly well had occurred, should be classified as an unimportant aberration and forgotten. She could not deny what happened to her, but because she was already committed to a doctrine that has no place for any transcendent reality whatever she did not even consider giving her experience a religious interpretation. Wesley, of course, did. Immediately after the sentence about the strange warming of his heart, he writes of being given the assurance that God "had taken away *my* sins, even *mine*, and saved *me* from the law of sin and death." In one sense he already 'knew' that God saves and forgives; he had been taught this doctrine and had preached it himself. But after Aldersgate he *knew*. His notional apprehension of its meaning became a real apprehension.

To use the terminology proposed in this chapter, the assurance Wesley was given was faith; what he was assured of was the truth of doctrines with which he had long been familiar. He knew them by heart, in that he understood and could recite all the words. Now, he knew what he had been talking about—knew it, in the fullest sense, by heart. What I am suggesting is that in Wesley's case specifically religious doctrines came first in the chronological sense; what part they played in his conversion will be considered in the next chapter. For G.K. Chesterton, on the other hand, the biographical sequence followed the order of priorities I have set out in this section. Faith came first, religious doctrines later.

"I am the man," Chesterton writes, "who with the utmost

daring discovered what had been discovered before." With his usual wit, he compàres this feat with that of a yachtsman who, landing on the shore of what he had taken to be an unexplored island in the South Seas, finds that it is the country he was born in. The colossal native sculpture on which he plants the Stars and Stripes (I Americanize slightly) turns out to be the Statue of Liberty. Similarly, when Chesterton took stock of his deepest convictions and attempted to express what he felt in his bones was so, he found that he had invented for himself "an inferior copy of the existing traditions of civilized religion." As he would put it some years afterwards, "I have kept my truths: but I have discovered, not that they were not truths, but that they were not mine."

What truths? Briefly, that the world is not just a brute fact; it does not explain itself; it has a meaning and therefore has someone who means it. "There was something personal in the world, as in a work of art." Further, that in spite of its defects this work of art is beautiful, that it is something to be thankful for, and that the gratitude it elicits can only be "an obedience to whatever made us," a kind of humility and restraint. "These are my ultimate attitudes towards life," Chesterton concludes, "the soils for the seeds of doctrine." A mere list of these attitudes, shorn of their Chestertonian embroidery, cannot convey why he found them so compelling or how he arrived at them. The point is that he did, and that he did it on his own. The 'spirit of the age' gave him no encouragement; if anything, it was hostile to his homegrown truths. On the other hand, all of them were "things that I might have learnt from my catechism—if I had ever learnt it." Later, when he did learn it, thereby discovering that his original interpretation of the world was nothing of the kind, the ground had been prepared. His convictions were 'soils for the seeds of doctrine.'

The metaphor is apt. Sometimes doctrines, like seeds, can lie dormant for years, as seems to have been the case with Wesley; sometimes, as with Chesterton, they fall on fertile ground and take root rapidly. Usually, however, it is something in between. Not many people hammer out on their own a philosophy of life as articulate as Chesterton's, and of those who do, not many find that it coincides as neatly as his with 'the existing traditions of civilized religion.' Nor is every religious conversion, like Wesley's, a single jolt between before and after. A corner gradually turned, as with Augustine, is no less a corner. In any event,

> *Whether at once, as once at a crash Paul,*
> *Or as Austin, a lingering-out swéet skíll,*

being turned towards God is not coming to a standstill. It is a gift that does not become a possession. And since it is always given in particular situations to particular people with particular backgrounds, there are not only varieties of religious experience but also varieties of the faith to which that experience gives birth. However secure it may be, faith, like love, is never static. As there are stages in the cognitive and moral dimensions of human life, so too faith grows, deepens, and matures. As it does, the apprehension of doctrines that faith makes possible also changes. It need not be a derogation of childlike faith to point out that children grow up; on the contrary, doctrines can be accepted more wholeheartedly as they come to be understood more clearheadedly. An adult's world is different from a child's, and as it is in that world that the life of faith is lived, so too it is in relation to that world that doctrines have to be understood.

There is no explicit believing without some measure of understanding what one believes. On the other hand, while the judgment 'Yes, that is so' does exclude doubt, it does not automatically solve every puzzle and problem that religious doctrines entail. Augustine defined belief as 'pondering with assent,' and pondering means raising further questions. Without going back on 'Yes, that is so,' it is possible to ask, '*How* is that so?' Such a question can be prompted by the objections and arguments of others. But it can also be prompted by wonder, curiosity, that desire to know everything about everything which is intrinsic to the human spirit and which is one manifestation of the human desire for God. Those who have felt some twinge of this urge to understand may find in the rest of this book, if not answers, at least some hints worth pondering on their own.

❧ THREE ❧
Doctrines and Community

Usually the way must be made ready for heaven, and then it will come by some other; the sacrifice must be made ready, and the fire will strike on another altar.

CHARLES WILLIAMS

CONSIDER THIS CONUNDRUM: are you the same person you were fifteen years ago? The catch in the question is easy to spot. As stated, it can be answered either way, depending on how you understand 'the same.' Certainly you are the same person in the sense that you have always been yourself, not somebody else. In another sense, however, you are not at all the same as you were fifteen years ago, or fifteen days for that matter. Something has changed. The shape of your life as well as the shape of your body is different from what it was.

It is different because you have been changing it. You have set yourself goals that you succeeded or failed in reaching; you have formed or nurtured or broken habits and friendships, taken opportunities or passed them up, run into dead ends, made fresh starts. Who you now are, you have come to be through a cumulative series of decisions. Momentous or trivial, deliberate or thoughtless, wise or rash, the choices you have made have made you. What Ebenezer Scrooge says to the ghost in Dickens's *Christmas Carol* applies to every act of deciding, not just the dramatic ones: 'I am not the man I was. I will not be the man I must have been but for this intercourse.'

The Scrooge who lavishly dispenses cheer and poultry after making this resolve is in one sense none other than the Scrooge who, before making it, tyrannized his clerk and chased off carolers with a ruler. Yet making it gave the direction of his living, his character or way of life, a new turn. Similarly, one way to understand the conundrum proposed above would be to say that you are the same person you were fifteen years ago, but a different kind of person. You, nobody else, performed the thousands of conscious actions that lie between then and now, but by performing each of them you changed the performer, and so brought your present self into being. Not every corner is as sharp and noticeable as the one Scrooge turned. But changes are no less real for being gradual. You, like every other human being, have been and still are a person in the making.

That is the theme on which the present chapter will elaborate in several ways—to be human is to be in process of becoming. The first thing that needs to be added is that our making of ourselves is a personal, but for that very reason not an individual process. The distinction is important. By way of clarifying it, try to imagine for yourself what your day would be like if suddenly, overnight, you totally lost your memory.

You wake up to the sound of the alarm clock, only you do not remember what an alarm clock is or what it is for. It is not just that you have forgotten how to tell time; those squiggles—1, 2, 3, and so on—what are they? You look at your surroundings and draw a blank. They are just surroundings. You might as well be seeing them for the first time. So too with family and friends. Instinctively, perhaps, you recognize that they are somehow like yourself; otherwise, they are nameless strangers, unrelated, so far as you are concerned, either to yourself or to each other. Someone says 'Good morning' and you sense that the sounds you hear are an amiable gesture, but you do not understand them as words. Nor can you respond in kind, except by grunting, for you have forgotten how to speak.

I leave the reader to continue the exercise. There are two points to be drawn from it. The first amplifies what I have already said: without memory, you would be quite a different person, one without a past, cut off from all that you had become. Secondly, however, the past that would vanish consists in more than the sum of all your previous experiences. You would have forgotten as well what those experiences *meant*, how they fit together, what their significance was. Even more important, you would have forgotten all you ever knew about things beyond your own experience, all that you had been told, all that you had read about, all that had in any way been communicated to you by others—your birthday, the square root of nine, who the President is, what a coffeepot does. Not only, then, would you be quite a different person. Your world too would be quite a different world. It would be scarcely more than a kaleidoscope of unconnected sights and sounds with no order, unity, structure, or purpose; in short, no meaning or value. You would have reverted to something like infancy.

For the world that infants live in is no larger than their immediate environment. It includes only what they can feel and see and hear. Babies have no routines or responsibilities, no concern about the price of crude oil, no opinions on vitamin C or the Equal Rights amendment, no interest in Joan of Arc or Haley's comet. None of these is or can be real to them until they are talked into talking. Infancy ends when speech begins. Partly because nearly everyone has made the transition and partly because hardly anyone remembers making it, we tend to overlook how momentous a change it is. Even learning to read, watershed though it is, really amounts to an extension of something that children have already learned by learning to speak, namely that immediate experiences can *mediate*. Certain patterns of ink on paper are like certain patterns of sound, in that both are more than patterns. They mean something. And what they mean need not be immediate, present, here and now. That was what Helen Keller came to realize by a different and more striking route. For her, the breakthrough came when she grasped the connection between a particular set of sensations, the touch of her teacher's fingertips on her palm, and water. At that moment she began to enter a vast new world, a world that was not immediate but mediated, by language.

It is because that world is so vast and various that there is no single meaning of 'meaning.' To mean is to intend, designate, signify, communicate, refer, suggest, imply, think about, interpret, denote, connote, assert. Depending on the circumstances, you can use all of these verbs in place of 'mean.' A dictionary will tell you how to make the substitution correctly. Making it intelligently, though, is something else again. For that, you need more than an understanding of how the English language is used. You also have to understand what those who use it, yourself in particular, are doing when they intend, designate, signify, and so on. Meaning, in the dictionary sense of defining words verbally, is like rearranging furniture or replacing a couch with a sofa. It is purely formal, a mere diagram of meaning in the sense of being related to the real world. To put it another way, anyone who is capable of asking about the meaning of meaning already lives in such a meaningful world. The question itself presupposes that words, including the words the question is framed in, *do* mean.

Language is not the only vehicle or carrier of meaning, but it is the one that is most pertinent to the topic of this chapter. So far, I have proposed that each of us is a person in the making, that the world in which we constitute ourselves is a world of meaning as well as an environment of experience, and that we enter this lived world largely through the medium of language. Taken together, all of this suggests the main reason why the process of becoming human is not a private venture. Language is learned. By learning it we learn not only how to talk but also what there is to talk about. Your world is yours only because others have shared with you their own experiences and attitudes, insights and know-how, beliefs, views, information, hopes, biases, and wisdom. Apart from this inherited fund of meanings and values, you would have no mental capital to draw on, no way to lend coherence and purpose to your living. As it is, however, the simplest of everyday actions is one stitch within an elaborate fabric of meaning.

Consider, for instance, what is involved every time you mail a letter. Sticking a scrap of gummed paper on the envelope means that you believe it is a postage stamp of the right denomination for domestic mail, that you expect it to be recognized as such by the postal service, and that you are reasonably confident your letter will therefore be delivered in one piece to the right address before (say) the end of next month. On your commonplace action all the complex machinery of government, politics, transportation, and economics converge. Without them it would be less than trivial. It would be meaningless. Your stamp would be a specimen of the engraver's art, nothing more.

To pursue this last point, what is it that makes a cathedral a cathedral? There is no answer to be had by measuring its dimensions or describing its architecture or comparing it with other buildings. That would only specify it as a physical edifice. Even a discourse on its beauty would not explain why it is a cathedral rather than a lecture hall or a railway station. What makes it a cathedral is not observable appearance but meaning. It is a cathedral because of what it is for, what goes on in it, what the people who act in certain ways within its walls believe and love and hope for.

> *A serious house on serious earth it is,*
> *In whose blent air all our compulsions meet,*
> *Are recognised, and robed as destinies.*

Such a building is constructed by human hearts and minds as well as hands. Its most important components are not stone and mortar but conviction and feeling.

Meaning is a constituent of everything men and women build—their institutions, their relationships, themselves. A marriage is something more than monogamous mating because of the memories and expectations, the promises, plans, decisions, and assessments that define each partner in relation to the other. Even a marriage 'made in heaven' is remade day by day and year by year. The vows it starts with are interpreted in light of new situations; patterns of behavior are formed and reformed; affection finds new embodiments or withers for lack of them. Such a marriage may result in what the *Cynic's Word Book* defines as a community consisting of a master, a mistress, and two slaves, making in all, two. Or the two may be, in Chesterton's phrase, not twice one but ten thousand times one. In any case, how things turn out depends in the long run on how a man and a woman turn each other into husband and wife. By changing what their marriage means they change what it is.

Not that every marriage is invented from scratch. On the contrary. Matrimony is among other things a civil contract, and so part of its meaning derives from the way it is understood in law. Moreover, everyone who marries has some conception of what it is to be a spouse, what married life is like, how husbands and wives ought to behave towards their families, friends, and neighbors. Marriage, that is, has specific meaning within a larger society. How that society regards marriage as an institution will play a large part in determining the shape of particular marriages; they, in turn, will either reinforce the prevalent norms and expectations or alter them by embodying different ones. The 'ideal' marriage, in other words, is not an eternal archetype. It is a social construction, part of the world of meaning in which every adult learns to live.

From that world come the assumptions, attitudes, and expectations that for the most part we take for granted. What each of us thinks, not only about marriage but also about matters as deep as the human situation and as minor as the way to eat an oyster, depends very largely on what everyone else is thinking about them. That is why an urban Californian born and bred who moves to northern Maine is likely to experience at least a mild form of culture shock. He or she would be in a different world, surrounded by people who use the same English words and yet speak as it were a different language. The difference is no less real for being hard to pin down. Indeed it is hard to pin down because it has to do with real life. The habits, quirks, views, and routines that combine in a life style usually get no more attention than breathing does. Things are done in such and such a way because that is how things are done. The same goes for thinking: "You tell me whar a man gits his corn pone, en I'll tell you what his 'pinions is."

There is a paradox here. What I have called the lived world is the result of human insight, assessment, interpretation, and approval. As such it exists only in so far as people are conscious of it. If everyone woke up one day with the kind of utter amnesia that I asked the reader to imagine a few pages back, everything would grind to a halt. Artifacts of the human world would still exist. There would still be alarm clocks and airports, postage stamps and cathedrals. Only no one would have an inkling of what any of them was for. Nor would men and women know what *they* were for themselves. They would be overgrown infants. That is one side of the coin. The other is what I have just said about awareness of the human world as itself a product *of* that world. The process of being educated, socialized, and acculturated is a human process, yet it turns out the persons who run it. The structures of our world structure *us*. The 'system,' the set-up, the way things go, has a life of its own that is seemingly independent of the lives of those who keep it going. It is like a building that generates its own builders. And in this reciprocal process, as may already be evident, believing plays a very large part.

There is a story about someone who visited a zoo for the first time, noticed the giraffe, gazed at it for a while, and then said gravely, 'I still don't believe it.' An extreme case, no doubt, but an instructive one. Seeing, despite the proverb, is not always believing. Quite often it works the other way round. Our beliefs are the framework into which new experiences fit—or do not fit, as the case may be. A person who believes that demon-possession occurs will construe certain sorts of experiences and states of mind quite differently from someone who believes no such thing, but does believe that occasionally human beings go mad. Demons (but not psychoses) fit into one world, psychoses (but not demons) into the other. Which of these worlds corresponds to the universe as it actually exists is a question that would be extremely important in another connection, but not here. They are both 'real' worlds, in the non-technical sense I have been using, and they are both constituted by belief.

I suggested in the previous chapter that such beliefs, formally expressed, are doctrines. And doctrines in that general sense inform not only what we think about life but how we live it as well. To take a controversial example, there are people who hold that in the last resort men and women bear a personal responsibility for the choices they make. Others hold on the contrary that every act is entirely due to circumstances over which the agent has no control. The former accept a doctrine of free will; the latter, a doctrine of determinism. The fact that these two doctrines are incompatible has practical consequences, notably in medical jurisprudence. For while the institution of legal justice in this country is built on the premise that as a rule persons are to be held accountable for crimes they commit, a large part of the institution of psychiatry is built on the premise that as a rule they are not. Hence the protracted debate over the insanity plea.

My point, however, is not to take sides on what is on any showing a very tangled issue. It is simply that doctrines matter. One way or another, doctrine—about economics and politics, about what it is to know and what it is to love; in brief, about the best way to live—pervades everyone's world and provides much of its meaning. But notice that the important part of this last sentence is the opening phrase. Doctrine matters 'one way or another.' Mostly the way is indirect. Very few people take an explicit stand on any of the topics just mentioned. Most of us, most of the time, simply accept more or less uncritically the meaning and value of the world we grew up in, including its beliefs and doctrines. Often they are a very mixed lot. But that too is covered by a doctrine, the doctrine of 'live and let live' or, to give its more recent and formal name, the doctrine of pluralism.

2

This chapter is about community, and what I have said in the previous section leads to this preliminary definition: a community is a group of people who share meaning and value. To put it the other way round, wherever there are common understandings, common views, common beliefs or judgments, common expectations or goals, there is at least a rudimentary community.

This is admittedly a somewhat theoretical way to state what constitutes community, in the sense that it is hard to visualize. But that is deliberate. The word 'community' may conjure up the image of a town meeting, a family at supper, a lacrosse team, or what have you. And such a mental picture may well represent a community in the sense I have just defined. But a cluster is not necessarily a community. Passengers on a bus sit side by side, but they are a collection, not a community, unless their common experience has some common meaning. If they are all headed for the same taxidermists' convention, say, or the long-awaited appearance of a rock band, they may *become* a community, for a while anyway, in virtue of what their common destination means to them. Similarly, the tenants of an apartment building live close together, but if they meet to plan a barbecue they will have more in common than their landlord and they will have moved from mere collocation towards community.

Like persons, communities are constituted by meaning. It can be lived meaning, unspoken and unnoticed, as in casual communities such as neighborhoods, or institutionalized meaning, clearly defined in bylaws and organizational hierarchies, or something in between. Thus a family need not be a community, though often it is, and a bureaucracy can be a community though often it is not. Everyone knows of close relations who live mutually isolated in the same house. Blood may be thicker than water, but bloodlines by themselves do not draw people together. Neither does red tape. Yet even the most impersonal bureaucratic structures are not, strictly speaking. mechanical; they depend on human cooperation and decision, and to that extent they are not altogether meaningless.

From this definition, it follows that since communities depend on common meaning they weaken when meanings collide and collapse when meaning breaks down. Take for instance friendship, the community of two that Coleridge called a sheltering tree. The metaphor is a good one, for a friendship of long standing has not been standing still. It has grown. It means more than it did when it began, because both friends have gone on being human, and consequently have more to share. Such a friendship can withstand drought for a long time, but not indefinitely. Most people have had the sad experience of meeting an old friend, someone they have not seen for years, and finding that except for reminiscences there is nothing to say. Both parties have grown, but they have grown apart.

Or, take the demonstrations and strikes that erupted on many college and university campuses at the end of the 1960s. Everyone experienced them. Not everyone, however, understood the experience in the same way. Disagreement about the meaning of these events, and still more about their worth, not infrequently split whatever community had previously existed into 'us' and 'them' factions. In some places this breakdown of trust and respect has lasted ever since.

Or, finally, take what is sometimes called the global village. There is a real sense in which communication and transportation have shrunk our planet and made neighbors of the whole human race. But the twentieth century will also be remembered as a time of unprecedented disagreement on very basic issues, nuclear armament being the most obvious. The problem is not simply that it is hard to decide what is right and what is not. That has always been difficult. Rather, the problem is a chronic lack of agreement on how rightness is to be established in the first place, and even on whether it can be established. Such a situation makes it almost impossible to argue convincingly for any particular position, since arguing presupposes a common understanding of what the argument itself is about. It is not surprising, then, that the various groups and parties often do not argue. They shout. In that regard, the global village is a long way from being a world-wide community.

So far, from travelers on a bus to travelers on 'spaceship Earth,' my emphasis has been on community as the result of meaning shared in the present. But the sharing extends through time as well. The analogy that was suggested earlier between personal and social existence also applies here: every community, except the most evanescent, is what it is because of what it has been. What memory is to the individual, tradition is to community. Like persons, communities make themselves by building on what they have already made. Tradition, in the sense of transmitting or handing down, is one of the ways in which meaning is mediated and spread among many.

Any carrier of meaning can be part of this process. Gestures such as smiling, sending flowers, shaking hands, and saluting all have a meaning. Each is a means of communication. But what they communicate, how they are used, and when it is appropriate to use them are all matters of tradition. Language, which is in many ways the most important carrier of meaning, is itself a tradition. Parents hand it down to their children, and teachers to their students. Moreover, within the broad stream of tradition common to everyone who speaks English there are more or less distinct currents. British English and American English are different in grammar and idiom as well as vocabulary, though the difference is not usually so great as to cause serious misunderstandings. Adjusting from 'I haven't got any petrol' to 'I don't have any gas' or *vice versa* is comparatively easy. It is harder to learn the more differentiated languages of smaller and more specialized communities. Lawyers, for instance, use words among themselves in highly technical ways to express with precision the meanings that constitute the legal community. The same is true of scientists, coin collectors, and theologians. Because each of these particular languages is handed down in and by a community, those who stand outside such a tradition will probably find, as the bromide 'That's Greek to me' suggests, that much of what is said and written by those who stand within it is about as meaningful as γνωθι σαυτόν.

Inasmuch as human being is a cooperative project, tradition, in the sense I have been using here, informs every aspect of every human world. Deeds, like words, have careers behind them. Any activity in the present, from eating meals with forks and spoons to providing for those who have no such utensils and nothing to eat with them, represents the result to date of a process of transmission and adaptation. In that sense there are no dead traditions, only hollow or purely formal ones. Something that once was handed down but now has only historical interest is no longer a tradition; no longer, that is, part of any community's common meaning. Alchemy would perhaps be an example of this, though astrology would certainly not.

Thus the contrast often drawn between traditional societies and modern ones is misleading. Modernity itself is a tradition. To be sure, it is a tradition of uprooting, "a titanic and deliberate effort to undo by technology, rationality and governmental policy the givenness of what came down from the past." But the idea that what is new is bound to be better than what is old is not itself new. The doctrine of progress has a long tradition. Those who place originality and independent thinking higher on their scale of values than adherence to custom and convention are in fact adhering to one of the conventions of modernity by carrying on a particular tradition *about* tradition. 'So-and-so's views are traditional,' unless 'traditional' is being used to condemn or praise rather than describe, is almost a redundant statement. Everyone's views are traditional. The question is which tradition they belong to, and whether that tradition is worthy of praise or blame.

By asking such a question, individuals and groups ask who they are. Knowing yourself is becoming aware of what you have become, reflecting on the decisions which you have made and which have made you, and thus knowing yourself as responsible for the direction your life is taking. '*Why* am I doing all this?' leads inevitably to '*Should* I be doing all this?' The same thing happens in communities. Internal crisis or external challenge can move a community to take stock of itself, evaluate its common meaning, redefine its common goals. It has been said, for example, that children make a marriage; they can also unmake it. Everything depends on how a man and a woman assess themselves as husband and wife in light of their having become parents.

Assessments of this kind, furthermore, made by a community reflecting on its own tradition, become part of that tradition. When the proverbs and slogans that guide everyday life are scrutinized and sifted, the result is philosophy. When teaching and learning are similarly weighed, the result is educational theory. When literature and the arts are reflected on, the result is critical commentary. When religion is studied and evaluated, the result is theology, about which more will be said in the next chapter. And, in general, when the meanings that inform a society's common life are brought to light, the result is culture. Culture, as that word will be used here, refers to social self-awareness. It is an aspect of tradition that consists in reflection on other aspects, and a level of meaning at which a society becomes a deliberate society by taking responsibility for the meanings that constitute it. I have already said that what memory is to an individual, tradition is to community. Culture is community with a conscience.

The gist of the present section has been that personal existence is interpersonal, but it is also more than that. In chapter two I talked about that fulfillment of the human desire for meaning which comes from encountering a strange yet intimately personal love that puts everything else in a new light. And just as light takes its color from what it illuminates and shines through, so also religious conversion colors and is colored by particular human communities and is mediated by words and gestures, symbols and ceremonies, and everything else that expresses the belief and practice of a religious tradition. More especially, this love enters the shared world of common meaning through the lives of those who themselves believe and practice such a tradition. But in order to understand the particular religious community that is the Christian church, and what it has to do with doctrines, there is one more topic to be considered, which unites all that I have discussed so far. That topic is story.

3

The point of the imaginary attack of amnesia with which this chapter began was that without the past as an ingredient the present would have no form. But the present, the 'now' that we experience, is structured not only by memory but also by anticipation. It is not a dimensionless instant, a kind of razor's edge between a past that no longer exists and a future that is yet to be, but a span or stretch of time composed of expectations as well as recollections.

What I experience, for example, at any particular moment as I drive to work is not just a mélange of sights and sounds. It has a shape. It takes in memories so habitual that I do not attend to them, such as where the brake pedal is, and other memories that are more or less present to mind, such as the route I ordinarily follow in the morning. But each moment is also informed by anticipations—where I am going, what I will do when I get there, what the driver ahead of me is up to, what the consequence of changing lanes is likely to be, how much time is left before I arrive, whether it is important to be punctual today, and so on. The mixture changes from moment to moment, but there is a wholeness and continuity beneath the flux.

Similarly, a piece of music can be analyzed into a succession of chords, each of them built out of distinct tones, yet what we hear is something quite different. The piece as experienced is a melody or song or theme. Each note is related to what came before and at the same time it structures the listener's anticipation of what is coming next. In fact, music might almost be defined as distilled time. In it the temporal dimension that is present in all our waking experience (and in our dreaming as well) takes perceptible shape as a sequential pattern of sounds.

Only the present truly exists. But as Augustine observes in a famous passage of his *Confessions*, it exists in three ways. There is "a present time of past things; a present time of present things; and a present time of future things." Together they give the present, 'now' as it is experienced, its content of meaning and value and purpose. And thus, as Augustine well knew, our experience of ourselves and our world has a *narrative* quality.

It is a quality you have probably noticed if you have ever told a story, and almost certainly if you have ever tried to write one. The activity of writing is itself a sequence of events in time, in that you push the pen across the page or tap one typewriter key after another, but sequence alone is not narrative. If the words on paper are to have meaning as a story, you the writer must have in mind not only what you are writing at the moment but also what you have written already and what you are going to write. If you gave a certain character blue eyes in the first chapter, you had better not make them brown when you get to the fourth. And you had better not set the scene in an Arizona desert if your plot calls for a blizzard later on. In this respect, every 'now' in your act of writing is analogous to the 'now' of every act of living. Each is the present time of past things and future things as well as of present things. That may also be the overall shape of the story you are writing, if you arrange the events to follow one another in the order of their occurrence in time. Yet the same kind of arrangement appears in chronicles and annals, which are not strictly speaking stories at all. A chronology of events is not a narrative unless it also has a direction, a storyline, a plot that unfolds in and through the temporal sequence. A story, properly so called, goes somewhere–though just where it is going may not be apparent until the last chapter.

There is of course an important difference between writing a story and living a life. Novelists can write whatever suits their fancy, and they can go back and revise what they have written in order to iron out inconsistencies. By contrast, there is no way to undo what has already happened in real life, and very little of what has yet to happen can be decided in advance. Yet this contrast is not absolute. The past that becomes an ingredient of the present through memory consists not of bare events but of meaningful events. What we remember are the things that have a bearing on the present and the future. This works two ways. On the one hand, the fact that we do remember something implies that it has been and still is important in some way. The people who have had an impact on our lives continue to have it in so far as we remember what they did and said. On the other hand, however, we may not realize the significance that some particular event or person has had for us until, perhaps long afterwards, new events prompt us to recall the past and discover how it fits into an emerging pattern of meaning. Much of modern psychotherapy aims at bringing to light forgotten episodes that nevertheless have an influence on the present.

That is why Augustine's discussion of time, mentioned above, is part of the book that has been called the first and greatest autobiography. The *Confessions* represent Augustine's effort to know himself, what he had become, by remembering what he had already been coming to be. In order to make present his own past, he tells a story that is anything but a dispassionate, blow-by-blow chronicle of everything that had ever happened to him. He could not have done that in any case, and it would have been pointless even if he could. From beginning to end his account of himself is selective; what he chooses to narrate is what was, in the light of subsequent developments, important. That he once stole some pears, for example, might seem too trivial an incident to record. Yet for Augustine himself it held, in retrospect, the seeds of later actions and disclosed motivations that were far from trivial. In one sense his childish prank had already happened; in another, equally real, and more important sense it was still happening. By recalling it as one scene of a single, coherent drama Augustine was discovering the process of his own becoming. But his act of self-discovery was as much a part of that process as his earlier act of stealing pears, and thus Augustine the man was changing as well as knowing himself by recalling Augustine the boy. Having brought to light the story out of which he had been living, he went on to live out of a different story.

For much of his adult life, it had been the story of a teacher of rhetoric. Augustine, to modernize a bit, was a professor. He molded his life on that model, taking up certain attitudes, cultivating certain acquaintances, holding certain views, and in general doing whatever teachers of rhetoric did. It might be said that he adopted a certain role, were it not that 'role' usually suggests something artificial, whereas what Augustine adopted— and what each of us adopts—was not a superficial mask. Being a friend is as much a role as being a Freemason, in this one crucial sense: it is something to be learned, experimented with, and practiced.

The same is true of other ways of being human. Each of us by a thousand actions, great and small, is becoming someone, some particular kind of man or woman, by experimenting with at least one story and probably with several. There is only one edition of the story each of us is composing, and we make it up as we go along, yet what we are making is for the most part a variation on some theme that has been heard before. An actress, for example, can abandon the role she has been playing, once the curtain goes down or she is no longer on camera, but she does not thereby abandon the role of an actress. Acting on a stage in dramas written by somebody else is part of one way to live the personal drama of human existence. Those who choose it do not 'become' Lady Macbeth, say, except in a figure of speech, but playing Lady Macbeth may be one of the things they do in becoming actresses who specialize in Shakespeare. The niche they carve has been carved already.

And what is true of being an actress is true of being a parent, a sales representative, a neighbor, a birdwatcher, a citizen, a jogger, or an Australian: we learn what it is to *be* any of these by encountering the appropriate actions and feelings, manners and mannerisms, embodied in the real or imagined stories of parents, sales representatives, joggers, and so on. Deliberately or (more likely) without being aware of it, we make our own stories out of the stories of others. Thus, in general, the saying is quite correct. Everyone does turn into what he or she is masquerading as. What seems like imposture at first eventually becomes second nature. "The distinction between pretending you are better than you are and beginning to be better in reality is finer than moral sleuth-hounds conceive."

For all these reasons, as Augustine realized, the question 'Who am I?' is equivalent to 'What is my story?' When we speak of someone's self-fulfilling prophecies, we are pointing to the fact that people construe their worlds to conform with the stories they have cast themselves in. A person who experiences a 'midlife crisis' is discovering that the story he or she was living is not turning out as it should. The American Dream, like every other dream, has a story line—flexible, adaptable, but nonetheless recognizable. Textbooks in primary schools teach more than reading; they teach meanings and values, indirectly, by telling stories. Television is now the narrative medium *par excellence*. It presents those who watch it with stories that display a whole range of goals for the human project. Those who object to televised episodes of sex and violence are merely pointing out two conspicuous trees in a vast narrative jungle. Even the commercials are carefully and deliberately crafted stories that end, more or less overtly, 'And they lived happily ever after. So can you, if you buy Our Brand.'

It is a long way from Augustine to advertising, but the point has been the same all along. As our lived experience has a narrative quality, so too it is concrete narrative rather than abstract argument that affects our living most deeply and lastingly. Stories are the most persuasive carriers of personal meaning. They give us our world. Thus I began this chapter by proposing that the human world is mediated, and in large measure constituted, by human acts of understanding, judging, believing, and loving. Those meanings become most real to us when they are bodied forth in particular human agents who take part in particular stories. Again, I have said that community exists wherever, and in so far as, meanings and values are held in common. To that it can now be added that a community is a group with a common story. We become members of a community by adopting its story as our own, and equally we adopt a story by becoming part of a community.

This last point can be made by referring to the specific community of natural scientists. In chapter two I had occasion to note that scientific knowledge is largely a matter of belief. It is not, in other words, the property of any individual scientist but of a group. From what has been said in this chapter, it should be clear that both this shared knowledge and the sharing of it serve to make this group a community. Since a comparatively high level of agreement on what they do and do not know is normal among scientists, theirs is a comparatively more cohesive community than others. But besides knowledge, scientists share commitments and goals. Science has been called the art of the soluble, and for the most part scientists agree that the best solutions take the form of the generalizations known as laws, that thoroughness and accuracy are desirable in arriving at these generalizations, and so on.

Yet all of this, as stated, is abstract. Concretely, one becomes a scientist in the same way Augustine became a professor of rhetoric—by behaving like one. Would-be scientists serve an apprenticeship that is none the less real for being informal. They learn what it is to be a graduate student, what steps have to be taken in order to get the academic degree that serves as their union card, which journals to subscribe to and publish in, how a laboratory or field expedition runs, what to be enthusiastic about, what sorts of jobs are worth seeking, which associates it would be well to become acquainted and if possible friendly with—all this, and more, they learn by discovering and appropriating the plot of a scientist-story. Which is simply to say that while scientific knowledge can be and is pursued for its own sake, those who pursue it are human. Their rather closely knit community exhibits many of the same characteristics as do other groups, professional and amateur alike. Communities are built around stories.

4

Throughout this chapter I have been approaching one and the same complicated reality from different angles. I have considered the process of being human as living in a world, as participating in a community, as passing on a tradition, as enacting a story. All of these, as I suggested earlier, bear on being human in relation to transcendence. While almost none of my examples has as yet been drawn from religious community in general or the Christian community in particular, everything I have said so far does apply to the church. The Christian community is, though it may be more than, a human community.

It can be objected that such an approach to understanding the church is at best marginally relevant. Christian community ought to be understood as what it understands itself to be—the fellowship of the Holy Spirit, perhaps, or the communion of saints, or a 'new creation by water and the word.' Alternatively, the starting point should be the four distinctive 'marks of the church,' its oneness, holiness, universality, and apostolicity, rather than general human categories. The latter (so the objection runs) can only lead to a reductionistic view from which everything unique and special about the Christian community would be missing.

The premise of this objection is sound, the conclusion only partly so. How a community understands itself is part of its common meaning, and therefore part of what it *is*. Thus to omit this shared self-understanding does lead to incompleteness and distortion. But from this premise it does not follow that the meanings which are peculiar to a community are the only ones that make it what it is. In fact, such a conclusion tends towards reductionism of another sort; in the case of Christian community, towards an understanding of the church so exclusively churchly as to have no relation to the way anything else is understood. The result may well be internally consistent, but then so is a crossword puzzle. Even ecclesiologists, who specialize in understanding the church, may begin to wonder if they are talking *about* anything.

To put it another way, the 'marks' or 'notes' of the church that I have mentioned are doctrines. So are the assertions that the church is the communion of saints, the fellowship of the Holy Spirit, and the like. Together with its other teachings, the church's doctrine about the church is part of what constitutes it as the sort of community it is. Equally, however, part of what makes these doctrines the sort of doctrines they are is the fact that they express the church's common understandings and judgments about itself. This community and these doctrines define one another.

This last sentence sums up the main point of the present chapter: there is a reciprocal relation between the particular community which is the church, and the particular meanings and values reflected in its doctrines, including its doctrine of the church. My reason for postponing this thesis until now is that doctrines and community need to be understood not only in relation to each other but also within the broader context sketched in the previous three sections. The church is a community of doctrine, defined by what it teaches, but what it teaches has a place in the larger world of human meaning. In ways that will be discussed in the next four chapters, its doctrines influence and are influenced by the beliefs and assessments that are handed down in other communities.

To take a fairly obvious example, going to church has been at times, and in some places still is, one of the commonly accepted social values. Nearly everyone does it, partly, perhaps mainly, because everyone else does. Even when regular churchgoing has ceased to be the norm, it often survives in the attenuated form of a preference for being married in and buried from a church building. Conversely, religious community can be the repository of values that are held to be important for society in general. Thus the Declaration of Rights adopted in 1774 by the Commonwealth of Massachusetts declares in stately phrases that:

> As the happiness of a people, and the good order and preservation of civil government, essentially depend upon piety, religion, and morality; and as these cannot be generally diffused through a community but by the institution of the public worship of God, and of public instructions in piety, religion, and morality: Therefore ... the people of this commonwealth have a right to invest their legislature with power to authorize and require ... the institution of the public worship of GOD.

'Instructions in piety, religion, and morality'—doctrines—were for the framers of the Declaration an essential constituent of civil community, and the meeting house on the green in many a Massachusetts town is a visible reminder that the goals of church and commonwealth were once partly identical in law as well as in fact.

Nor has 'civil religion' disappeared in the United States owing to the constitutional separation of church and state. Churches still observe national holidays like Thanksgiving and Independence Day, representatives of religious communities are invited in rotation to invoke a blessing upon school graduations, and so on. Much has changed in the thirty years since an incumbent President opined that "without God, there could be no American form of government, nor an American way of life." Yet on the whole it is still fair to say that "American religion and American society would seem to be so closely interrelated as to make it virtually impossible to understand either without reference to the other."

Examples of how religious meanings interlock with those of political, cultural, and economic communities might be multiplied indefinitely, for as many sociologists rightly maintain, religion is *the* social fact. From their point of view its main function is one of drawing individuals into community, by providing a 'sacred canopy,' a tradition of beliefs which covers every aspect of the world of lived experience and which enables those who share it to see life steadily and see it whole. Otherwise stated, religion fulfills the human desire for meaning. Belonging to a religious community gives one a place and a purpose in a world that makes sense. To the extent that other communities do the same, they can be regarded as providing a functional equivalent of religion. The cult of Wagnerian music, with its saints and its priesthood, its shrine at Bayreuth, its doctines and scriptures, is one frequently cited example; another and rather different one is the all-inclusive framework of meaning that the Communist party provides in China.

This leads to the further question of what, if anything, makes religious community more than a social fact. More specifically, what makes the church a religious as well as a human community? An answer has already been suggested, implicitly, in chapter two: the church differs from other communities partly in that it exists both as a result and for the sake of transforming love. For such a personal transformation is not private, precisely because it is personal. It eases that deepest of all human yearnings, the desire to be *for* someone else, to be acknowledged and cherished and accepted, to know that we count in the eyes of another person, to be known as intimately as we know ourselves; in a word, the desire to be special—not because we feel that we are not special but because we feel that we are, and cannot feel otherwise. To recognize this inner loneliness, as my colleague Sebastian Moore puts it, is to become aware of being one side of a conversation, a communication addressed 'To whom it may concern.' Whom it does concern we have to find out, or cease to be human. One way or another, the desire to be *for* another motivates all our living. The saddest of disappointments is the discovery that

someone we had counted on to be that other turns out to be a
stranger, unable (or, worse, unwilling) to carry on the conversation as far as it can go.

Yet that would seem to be what happens even in the most
intimate human relationships. They assuage our longing up to a
point, never completely, because what we long for is someone
to whom all hearts are open, all desires known, and from whom
no secrets are hid; someone who is no stranger; someone in whom
all the qualities of understanding and love that we feel in ourselves
are absolutely real. Our inner loneliness, in other words, is a
desire for God. "The very thing that makes us want to be for
another is destined to be forever unknown *by* the other," unless
the other is one who accepts us, simply and without qualification,
as we are. The strange warming of the heart that turns us towards
such an Other was discussed in the previous chapter; here the
point to be stressed is one that Moore makes.

> Now one may perhaps conclude, from the fact that our central
> desire is not totally fulfillable through human relationships but
> only in commitment to God, that we should seek fulfillment in
> this commitment rather than in human relationships. No conclusion
> could be more erroneous. On the contrary, the effect of experienc-
> ing the more radical fulfillment of our desire to be-for (in God) is
> that one will experience that desire more intensely in relation to
> other persons.

The love of God does not replace but rather enhances love of
neighbors. That is, it creates community. Hence the first part
of the specification I suggested earlier, namely that the church
in particular and religious communities in general exist as a result
of religious conversion. That such a statement cannot stand
alone, however, almost goes without saying. Both the church's
common life and its corporate action in society have at times
provided all too much evidence for motivations other than love.

But that leads to the second and more important part of my
specification: the church exists for the sake of conversion.

Religious experience itself is immediate. It happens. But as I have already suggested, all human experience has the quality of narrative. Its ingredients are past and future, memory and anticipation, both of which give meaning to what would otherwise be utterly unconnected feelings, thoughts, and sensations. What we experience, we experience *as* something or other. Religious experience is no exception. It occurs in some context, some meaningful world, structured by language, tradition, and community.

How the immediate experience and the mediated world of meaning are related is a subtle and much debated question. On one hand, even giving it the name 'religious' presupposes a shared language in which that word has more or less definite connotations. Had John Wesley grown up in a world from which religious meaning was totally absent, it is fair to speculate that he would have understood his experience quite differently. He might have paid no attention to it, or shrugged it off as unimportant. As it was, he construed it in the light of a particular tradition, handed down in a particular community. He was ready for it when it happened.

On the other hand no particular sort of background, however steeped in religious language, can guarantee that a transformation like Wesley's will happen at all, still less that it will happen in any particular way. Nor can any amount of ignorance or hostility prevent it. You never know when you are going to fall in love, or where, or with whom. It happens. So does the love of God. It happens to persons, and therefore it happens in the midst of the lived world of community and tradition. But it does not depend on any one configuration of that world. "Usually the way must be made ready for heaven, and then it will come by some other; the sacrifice must be made ready, and the fire will strike on another altar." It seems only reasonable that even if kindling cannot ignite itself it will nevertheless be more likely to catch fire if it is dry, but the metaphor is misleading. Human hearts are not made of wood, and the warming that transforms them is not a chemical process like combustion. Strictly speaking, it is not a natural process at all. It is a change that is out of all proportion to anything and everything that precedes it. Indeed, everything that precedes it is what changes. Conversion is not simply being turned around within a meaningful world: it is being turned towards "what no eye has seen, nor ear heard, nor human heart conceived, what God has prepared for those who love him" (1 Cor 2:9).

Yet conceived it must be—how otherwise can it affect the human world?—and the way in which it is conceived does much to determine how the church is understood. Thus Rosemary Haughton, in *The Transformation of Man*, distinguishes two main ways in which human life has been organized around the meaning of religious conversion. Because transformed existence, 'abundant life,' 'salvation,' the 'kingdom of God' is out of all proportion to ordinary living, it has sometimes been conceived as possible only outside the world of space and time; only after death, that is, and only in heaven. When salvation is thought of as a wholly future event, the result is what Haughton calls a 'formation community.' Such a community structures human life so as to prepare for the life of the world to come, by turning away from any worldly concern that might distract its members or endanger their hope of heaven, and by stressing the value of patience, training, and ascetic discipline. The regular and highly ordered life of some monastic communities offers an example, as do the practices of the Holy Club that the young John Wesley helped to found.

But the Christian tradition includes another way of understanding the converted life and a correspondingly different way of conceiving the church. For the 'community of the transformed,' to use Haughton's term, salvation is not a future event but one which has already occurred and which can be recognized by its spontaneous effects on the attitudes and behavior of those who have experienced it. Since they know at first hand that religious conversion is disproportionate to its antecedents, members of a 'community of the transformed' typically shun and condemn their former way of life.They draw a crisp line between the few who, like themselves, are manifestly saved and the many who manifestly are not; they require evidence of conversion as a condition of membership; they stress examination of their own consciences and those of others, not in order to prepare for transformation but in order to prevent backsliding. Such were the Donatists, a fourth-century community whose members held that since they had not defiled themselves by compromising with their pagan persecuters, they alone were truly Christians. And such were the seventeenth-century Puritans who sailed to America to found a 'city upon a hill,' untroubled by the corrupt and worldly church in England.

Both kinds of community have their characteristic blind spots. The first, the 'formation community,' tends to overlook the fact that transformation does occur in the present. The example Haughton uses is Benedict, who intended the monastic community he founded to be devoted to a corporate search for God. What he did not recognize clearly, because of the way he had learned to conceive salvation, was that he would not himself have been searching for God if God had not already found him. The idea that grace is a present reality as well as a promise and a hope was no doubt part of the tradition Benedict had inherited, but it had become submerged. Consequently it was not a major part of the formation for which alone the Benedictine monasteries existed, and like other such communities they slid gradually into tepidness, compromise with secular meanings and values, a tendency to be satisfied with their institutional structures, their buildings, and their traditions as holy in themselves rather than as a possible means to holiness.

The 'community of the transformed' is likewise prone to suffer from the defects of its virtues. From the fact that prior formation is irrelevant to conversion—which it is, strictly speaking—such a community infers that the human structures of community are likewise irrelevant to working out the consequences and implications of conversion—which they most

certainly are not. Where the 'formation community' is apt to overlook conversion here and now, the 'community of the transformed' is apt to enforce it here and now, by making its spontaneous effects the norm, which, as Haughton remarks, is like
making bread with nothing but yeast, or prolonging the feelings
of the honeymoon through the rest of a marriage. Because of the
black-and-white distinction it makes between the old life and the
new, there is little room in this kind of community for growth,
for stages in the development of faith, for gradually deepening
commitment. Those who are not yet converted will have to be
excluded altogether, or else forced to use a language that they are
not yet capable of understanding personally and thoroughly.

None of the examples mentioned so far is a pure case. There
are none. Transformation occurs in formation communities,
even though no one is looking for it this side of heaven; formation
is in practice an aspect of every community of the transformed,
even though everyone denies it in principle. Haughton's own
definition of Christian community strikes a balance. The church,
she writes, is "an educational structure with room for explosions." By education she means the whole complex process of
handing on a language in the broadest sense, a tradition of
expressed meanings and values that are compatible with (but not
necessary for) the explosions that remake those who have been
so educated. Since conversion is a reorientation of the whole
person, there is no aspect of the human world that is irrelevant
to such an education. If the meanings and values of secular society
are open to the possibility of transcendent love, then that society
is in fact, though perhaps not in intention, a religious 'formation
community.' Moreoever, if "religion is the organization of secular
life for sacred purposes," as Haughton puts it, then communities
other than the church can be, and sometimes are, more religious
than the church is.

Generally speaking, however, the tradition of modernity is
not notable for its openness to any inbreaking of the divine. On
the contrary. If the values that motivate a society or a culture are

grossly materialistic, if it excludes self-sacrifice, for example, or legitimates oppression, or ridicules asceticism, or in any of a thousand ways confines the goal of human living to what satisfies, then religious communities, unless they abandon what makes them religious, will have to duplicate secular structures or else seek to change them.

5

"What the church of Jesus Christ believes, teaches, and confesses on the basis of the word of God: this is Christian doctrine." So writes the eminent historian Jaroslav Pelikan at the beginning of *The Christian Tradition*, his magisterial account of what the church during the last nineteen hundred years has believed and taught and confessed. What I have suggested in the previous section is that his definition also works the other way round: where there is belief, teaching, and confession of Christian doctrine, there is the church. Both definitions are necessary. You cannot first single out a certain community, the church, and then examine it to discover what its doctrine is, because the church is in part a formation community, constituted by the doctrines it holds. But neither, on the other hand, can you first single out certain teachings, Christian doctrines, and then find a community that holds them, because they *are* Christian doctrines in so far as they constitute the church. Christian doctrine and Christian community are inseparable. Each defines the other, much as Germans can be defined as those who speak German, and the German language as what Germans speak.

This analogy is not merely formal. Christian doctrine is, in the broad sense, a language. It functions within the Christian community as a more or less coherent set of words and symbols that mediate Christian meanings and values and relate them to the rest of the human world. Handing on this language is what the church, as an educational structure with room for explosions, does. Doctrine, that is, pertains to formation. Its only purpose is

to make room for the explosions by making it possible to recognize them, articulate them, and sort out their meaning. The
doctrine of grace, for example, is about the explosions themselves:
"Grace is God's favor towards us, unearned and undeserved,"
and by giving it "God forgives our sins, englightens our minds,
stirs our hearts, and strengthens our wills." Neither in this formu-
lation nor in some more technical one does the doctrine as such
produce grace; that is part of what it means by saying that grace is
unearned. Yet it does describe what happens, and suggests that
when it does happen it is worth noticing and that it would be
worth learning more about whoever it is that makes it happen.

Thus every part of the formula just quoted leads to another
doctrine—to the doctrine of God as the giver of grace; to the
doctrine of revelation as what enlightens our minds; to doctrines
about who we are and where we come from, about what our sin
is and how it is overcome, about what our wills are strengthened
for, about the ultimate goal towards which we are drawn. Each
of these further doctrines has been particularized and elaborated,
formulated and reformulated, debated, defined, pondered, com-
mented on, translated, taught, believed, and lived. And the par-
ticularizing, elaborating, and so on are among the activities that
make the church a community.

So stated, however, the reciprocal interdependence of church
and doctrine might seem to imply that it does not matter much
what Christians say, so long as they say it in unison. 'Poor little
talkative Christianity,' as E.M. Forster called it, would in that
case be talking to itself. The church would be playing a language
game in which the words and the grammar constitute the players
as players, but do not necessarily mean anything outside it. The
only function of doctrines would be that they are, as a matter
of sociological fact, held in common.

Such a situation can arise. All too often it does. Doctrines
then become a cloud of verbiage, a code, a dead language that is
meaningful in the sense that it hangs together yet meaningless

in the sense that it appears to have no reference or relevance beyond itself. That, on the contrary, Christian doctrines do speak about something, I have tried to show in much of this chapter and most of the previous one. They say something about a turning or a transformation or a remaking which, for those who know it at first hand and take it seriously, puts everything in a new light, doctrines included. Only love is believable, and only 'love divine, all loves excelling' makes it possible to apprehend the meaning of Christian doctrines.

That is not, however, what makes them Christian.

Although I have written this chapter from a recognizably Christian point of view, only once has it referred to what distinguishes the church from other religious communities and gives its teachings their specifically Christian meaning. At the beginning of this section I quoted Pelikan's definition of Christian doctrine as what the church believes, teaches, and confesses 'on the basis of the word of God.' What this last phrase implies will be considered from different angles in the next four chapters. At present, what should be noted is this: the tradition by which Christians understand themselves and their community affirms that they have more to understand than their own experience. They have as part of their tradition a word, an address, a message which that tradition ascribes to God himself. Besides the immediate, 'inner word' of religious experience that addresses the heart, drawing men and women out of their loneliness into unspoken conversation with a transcendent Other, there is an 'outer word' that addresses them in the language of the human world of meaning. To call this the word of God is to say that through it God expresses himself. The channels of human speech and action, human thought and decision, convey meanings and values that have their source in him: his love is mediated as well as immediate.

The Christian community's belief that God really has spoken is the root of its conviction that its teachings are more than what could have been known apart from this word. Yet the word on

which Christian doctrines are based is not itself a doctrine. The
doctrines that define the church state the meaning of a message
that is first and foremost a story.

It was by telling a story that on the day the Christian community was established one of its members was moved to
announce publicly what that community was all about. What he
said was simple enough: a man who had recently been crucified
after performing certain remarkable deeds was now alive and was
pouring out extraordinary power on those who had known him
(Ac 2:22-36). So far as anyone can tell, the same story has been
the substance of the Christian message ever since—a story about
certain things that have happened and are having certain dis-
cernible effects. It was not a message claiming to be an original
philosophy or a new ethic. It claimed only to bear witness to
an event, the life and death and exaltation of Jesus of Nazareth.

Nothing else distinguishes the church from other communities. In so far as the meanings that constitute Christian community are specific to it, they are meanings embodied in the
story about this Jesus. The gift of the Spirit, grace, the love of
God—these are the names Christian tradition uses for an 'inner
word' that Christians share with others. What is distinctive about
Christianity lies in its 'outer word,' in the announcement that
the love of God meets human lovelessness in the human world,
through a particular person. His story is the core of a tradition
which, like other religious traditions, is cumulative. It has been
retold, embroidered, interpreted; conveyed in music and painting,
ritual and architecture; woven together with other stories. Above
all, his story has been embodied in the lives of men and women
for whom it has become *their* story, the source and expression
of their faith. Thus if there is anything specifically Christian
about the music of Palestrina or Purcell, it depends on this story.
If any Christian meaning remains in the festival of 'Xmas,' over
and above the sentiments connected with hearth and home and
holly, this story informs it. If there is a Christian moral code
or philosophy or world view, it is a working out of this story's

implications. If there are Christian families, Christian cultures, Christian churches, they are Christian to the extent that their structure and purpose, their memories and hopes, are rooted in this story.

Because the specifically Christian message takes the form of a narrative, the meaning is felt before it is figured out. Its meaning is not primarily informative, but affective, not a generalization about human life, but the drama of one particular life. Christians are those who realize what that drama means by forming their own stories in its pattern. In so doing, however, they also grasp and articulate what the message they have heard is about. And they do it together.

The story of Jesus, in other words, gives the Christian community a specific way of understanding religious conversion—the need for it, what it is like, what its results are, what is consistent with it. Learning this language is neither a necessary nor a sufficient condition of transforming love; what is learned is no more and no less than that it is the love *of* God *through* Jesus Christ and *in* the Holy Spirit. All the doctrines of Christianity are but explications of that one statement. But this is not to say that the Christian story itself is simply a symbolic way of expressing the character of religious conversion. It is that, certainly. It is a story about new life as a result of surrender, about the overcoming of all that separates and injures and destroys by what unites and heals and creates, about human loneliness transformed and human lovelessness forgiven. Yet there is more.

What happens to Christians, their community, and their world happens because of him whose story the Christian message proclaims. The good news of the gospel is not just that Jesus exemplifies the love of God but that he mediates it, that through him sins are forgiven, minds enlightened, hearts stirred, and wills strengthened. Above and beyond what it discloses about living in relation to transcendent mystery, the gospel presents itself as a disclosure of that mystery. Similarly the doctrines that the

Christian church has taught, believed, and confessed on the basis of this word do more than constitute the church as a religious community. By explaining what the Christian story means, they purport to be statements about its author, a God who loves without limit and who offers himself to be loved.

From the story they live by, Christians have learned who this God is and what he is doing to reconcile the world to himself. What they have learned, their community teaches in the two peculiarly Christian doctrines of the Trinity and the Incarnation. Both have implications for every aspect of human existence. Neither can be resolved into a generalization about human existence. Each depends on God's having entered the world of human meaning, thereby taking part in the human project, our making of ourselves.

And is it true, this story? Answering that question is not a matter of working out a sum. Everything depends on who is asking it. Finally, when all is said, the Christian story evokes one of two responses. You either love it or you hate it. Those who find themselves moved by its message, however tentatively, will go on to ask what it means and whether it is true in a manner quite different from those who find themselves repelled, and they will approach Christian doctrines differently.

❦ FOUR ❧
Doctrines and Authority

Humanity does not pass through phases as a train passes through stations: being alive, it has the privilege of always moving yet never leaving anything behind. Whatever we have been, in some sort we are still.

C.S. LEWIS

ACTIONS MAY SPEAK louder than words: they do not always speak so clearly. As a case in point, take the situation portrayed in a cartoon that appeared a few years ago. A schoolgirl is shown performing an interpretive dance while her classmates watch intently. Emerging from each child's head is the kind of bubble that cartoonists use to designate thinking. The dancer has in mind the image she wants her dance to depict—a tree. But the balloons above the rest of the class show that to one of them her actions suggest a bird, to another a sunrise, to a third a snowflake, and so on. The dance means something different to each of them—something other than a tree.

'Body language' does convey our moods and attitudes, often more eloquently than we realize. When it comes to expressing ideas or information, however, physical gestures are prone to ambiguity. As a means of communication, dancing has its drawbacks. Honeybees, it seems, do use a kind of dance to report the whereabouts of new and promising flowerbeds, but no human community has been known to share its knowledge choreographically. All of them use a more specialized and versatile set of bodily motions, coordinated movements of lips, tongue, and larynx, in order to produce a variety of audibly distinct sounds; these, in turn, combine to form the enormous number of discrete units which are spoken words. Substituting visible signs for articulate noise makes even further differentiation possible. There is virtually no limit to the number of distinctions and refinements that written language can express. Those who share its conventions can, for example, make it clear to each other that what they mean is not a snowflake but a tree; not just any tree, but more exactly a chestnut tree; and not just any chestnut, but one in particular, the spreading one under which the village smithy stands.

Words, spoken and especially written, are the most precise carriers of human meaning. Not that precision is everything. Words are weaklings compared with symbols, especially the primordial images that speak to us, in C.G. Jung's phrase, with a thousand trumpets. Language draws clear distinctions; symbols, as the derivation of the term suggests, 'throw together.' They communicate on different levels, unite several meanings, and evoke feelings as well as thoughts, all at the same time. In this richness lies their power. Still, language can do what symbols cannot: it can help in sorting out what symbols mean. The impact of the thousand trumpets is a direct, elemental communication; later on in a reflective moment we may wonder what has been communicated, and how. And the answer to such a question is not alternative symbolism, but an interpretation. To interpret a symbol is to go beyond it, to a different *kind* of meaning, expressed more clearly if less movingly in words.

Such a verbal explanation cannot take the place of the symbol whose meaning it unravels. Nor can the elemental meaning of symbols, certainly not the primordial images to which Jung refers, be exhausted by any amount of cool interpretive prose, however brilliant or insightful it may be. Why then make the attempt at all? Because, as Emerson's pithy remark has it, 'We are symbols and we live in symbols.' Each of us has his or her identity in a world of meaning, a world that is both 'thrown together' and shared largely by means of symbolic language. By understanding that language, we understand ourselves as the products and producers of a way of life, and what we understand we can more intelligently and responsibly change.

Thus interpreting the symbols that inform our personal and social being is an instance of the kind of reflection on meaning that was discussed in the previous chapter. There I suggested that every community is an ongoing process of sharing ideas, values, and beliefs, and that the process folds back on itself when a community begins to examine and evaluate the meanings it lives by. Every group and movement sooner or later finds it necessary to make such a self-assessment. The church is no exception. Christian community lives by the meaning embodied in a story. The story calls for its own publication, and telling it is what the church, as 'an educational structure with room for explosions,' is for. But if the meaning of the Christian story is to be communicated to all sorts and conditions of men and women, it will have to be told in as many different ways as there are audiences to hear it, for what speaks to the condition of one group may be cryptic and mystifying to another. Anyone who has tried to tell a family anecdote to a stranger knows the problem. Among family members, 'Cousin Pat has been at it again' may be all the introduction that is needed, but before anyone else could get the point a lot of background would have to be filled in. Getting the point of the Christian message across is made all the more complicated by the fact that the language of the story which embodies it, like all religious language, is allusive, metaphorical, and symbolic. If the same point is to be made in different words, chosen to suit a particular audience, what the point *is* had better be understood as clearly as possible. Those who would interpret Christianty to others need to know what it means.

Hence theology.

Christian theology is not the Christian story, though it is partly a reflection on that story. Nor is it preaching, though it exists partly for the sake of preaching and every other means of communication that contributes to Christian formation. Since formation itself exists for the sake of transformation, in the way that was outlined in chapter three, theology stands at two removes from religious conversion. If formation were not itself important—

if it did not matter what Christians said—theology would be superfluous. And since formation, strictly speaking, is neither a necessary nor a sufficient condition for the heart's being strangely warmed, the same goes for theology. The Spirit blows where it will. Nobody was ever saved by a theological treatise. Theologians only fill the gaps between the mystics.

Yet theology does have its uses. From the church's standpoint it is a clean-up operation. Theologians scrutinize, arrange, and sift the Christian tradition. They ask how Christians have interpreted the message they live by, how they are interpreting it, and how they can and should interpret it. Their work is a mirror in which the Christian community examines itself, its presuppositions and goals, what it has become and what it is becoming.

Not that theology is just an in-house operation. Christian community lives and always has lived in the midst of some social and cultural milieu, surrounded by other communities that live by other meanings and values. Because the traffic between religion and culture flows in both directions, even theologians who have one foot firmly and deliberately planted in the church cannot help having the other in these larger surroundings. Such a mediating stance allows, however, for a great variety of postures. More than a few theologians have been sharply critical of the church, and the church has disowned more than a few theologians. In North America, where for the most part the church and the university are institutionally separate, theologians have tended to identify themselves with the academic community.

But there is no need to rank theologians according to ecclesiastical loyalty, as though they were eggs to be graded. I am more interested in what they do. The gist of what I have said so far is that theology stands to religion as political science does to government, or economics to business and commerce. All three are specialized intellectual enterprises that aim to understand, assess, and promote activities that are already going on. Like other specialists, therefore, theologians often use a terminology of their own, and to that extent they form a community more or less distinct from others. Theological language can be complex and highly technical, and it sometimes suffers the fate of other refinements of everyday language, being regarded with suspicion by those who are not in the know.

Theologians no doubt grind out a lot that is merely academic. But, on the other hand, if the personal transformation that is the heart of religion alters a person's whole being in all its inter-personal, social, political, and intellectual dimensions, then any understanding of what it is to be human will be incomplete and probably distorted if it leaves religion out. And from this it follows that theologians do the object of their studies no honor by declining to aim for the same level of sophistication that has been achieved in the disciplines which study other aspects of human existence. It is true that theology, once 'queen of the sciences,' has lost her crown. There is no call for her to lose her head.

I opened this chapter by raising the problem of interpretation, and I have gone on to suggest that theologians have an interpre-tive role. They regulate the meaning of a religion by bringing its tradition to light, discriminating between what is essential and what is not, and assessing its value. Should anyone object that with so broad a definition the likes of Freud and Marx were theologians, well, so they were. Each aimed to understand the role of religion in Western culture. Their interpretations of Chris-tianity may be questionable: they are not flippant. Both have deeply affected the way Christian doctrine is understood today, by those who profess it and those who scorn it alike. If for no other reason, the church needs to take them seriously.

This in turn raises a question that will run through the present chapter and into the next. If Christian belief is neither infantile regression or the opium of the people, what is it? How can an interpretation that presents what is genuinely Christian be dis-tinguished from one that distorts or trivializes the meaning of

the Christian message? Which are the doctrines that do express
what the Christian community believes? How is such a decision
to be made, and who is to make it?

2

I have just raised the question of authority. Before I pursue
it, a distinction should be drawn between two senses in which
authority can be said to have a place in religion. In so far as the
church is an institution, it exercises authority in the sense of
setting conditions for membership. In so far as it is a community
of belief, one of these conditions may be the acceptance of
certain doctrines, stated in a creed or confessional formula. But
such theological tests, as Austin Farrer says, "are no more the
cause of faith than medical tests are the cause of health." The
institutional authority that requires an avowal of belief as one
qualification for belonging to the community is not the kind of
authority that makes doctrines believable in the first place. It is
only with authority in this second sense that I am here concerned,
but two further comments are in order. First, when a Christian
community does as a matter of polity require that its members
profess a set of beliefs, it is acting on a belief *about* those beliefs,
namely that those beliefs are what its common life is all about.
Thus authority in the second sense, the warrants and criteria for
believing, overlaps in practice with authority in the disciplinary
sense.

My second comment is that owing to this overlap, 'authority
for belief' can be confused with 'power that forces belief.' Short
of brainwashing, though, there is no such power.

> *He that complies against his will*
> *Is of his own opinion still.*

No one believes solely because institutional polity demands it,
although one of the motivations for genuine believing may be

the belief of a community that is a community of love as well as of belief.

So the question I raised at the end of the previous section returns: what does the Christian community believe? What counts as authentically Christian doctrine? Raising these questions almost invariably invokes the name of a fifth-century theologian, Vincent of Lérins, most of whose fame rests on the pithy and quotable answer he came up with. What counts as Christian doctrine, according to Vincent, is what has been believed everywhere, always, and by all; *quod ubique, quod semper, quod ab omnibus*. Between right doctrine on one hand, and teachings that are inadequate, deviant, or downright false on the other, the triple test of universality, antiquity, and consent draws a firm line.

Vincent's is a solidly conservative position. By itself, his threefold rule seems to equate error with innovation as such. In certain circumstances, however, Vincent does allow for the possibility of change, though only in the sense that there can be new interpretations of what everyone has always and everywhere believed. The Christian message itself is valid for all times and places, and thus the bulwark of the Vincentian rule is that this message has been handed down, whole and entire, from age to age.

Moreover, Vincent's appeal to tradition was part of the tradition he appealed to. Four hundred years before, Paul had declared that anyone, even an angel, who preached a gospel different from the one that he himself had handed down deserved to be *anathema*, denounced and cut off, and he made a point of insisting that what he was handing down was the same message handed down to him (Gal 1:8-9; 1 Cor 15:3). Similarly, a year or so after Vincent's death, several hundred bishops assembled at Chalcedon drew up a statement of Christian doctrine which asserts that they were endorsing what had been handed down to them, nothing else, and goes on to anathematize those who

teach the contrary. Since Paul's summary of the Christian message
and the definition of Chalcedon, as it is known, both profess to be
'handed down,' it will be instructive to compare them. Paul
writes as follows:

> *And now let me remind you of the gospel, which I preached
> to you, which you received, in which you stand, by which
> you are saved, if you hold fast to the message I preached—
> unless you believed in vain. For I handed down to you as of
> first importance what I too received:*
>
>> *that Christ died for our sins in accordance with the
>> scriptures,
>> that he was buried,
>> that he was raised on the third day in accordance with
>> the scriptures,
>> and that he appeared to Cephas, then to the Twelve
>> (1 Cor 15:1-5).*

Four centuries later, the bishops at Chalcedon declared:

> *Therefore, following the holy fathers, we are united in teach-
> ing all to acknowledge:*
>
>> *one and the same Son, our Lord Jesus Christ,
>> the same, complete in divinity, and the same, complete
>> in humanity,
>> truly God and truly man . . .*
>>
>> *the same, of one substance with the Father as regards
>> his divinity,
>> and the same, of one substance with us as regards his
>> humanity;
>> like us in all respects except for sin . . .*
>>
>> *one and the same Christ, Son, Lord, Only-begotten,
>> recognized in two natures,
>> without confusion, without change, without division,
>> without separation;*

*the distinction of natures being in no way annulled by
the union . . .*

*even as the prophets from earliest times spoke of him,
and our Lord Jesus Christ himself taught us,
and the creed of the fathers handed down to us.*

This is about half of the Chalcedonian definition, the full text of
which is given in the appendix, but it is enough for purposes of
comparison. Like Paul in his letter to the church at Corinth,
the bishops are saying something about Jesus Christ. How they
say it is something else again. Whereas Paul rehearses the climax
of the Christian story, there is scarcely a line of narrative any-
where in the definition of Chalcedon. It states, in a rather technical way, who and what Christ is, and stresses again and again
that what it is stating applies to *the same* Christ and not (we
may infer) to different ones.

Between Chalcedon's doctrine and Paul's, then, there is
clearly a difference of manner. Is there a difference of matter
also? Or are they different expressions of the same meaning,
the meaning of what has been believed everywhere, always,
and by all? I am less interested at present in the answer to this
question than in the question itself. For the doctrines I have
just quoted are only two among thousands that make up the
written tradition of Christian teaching, and so the question as
I have posed it can be generalized by asking whether this tradition is coherent. Is it a whole, internally consistent and unified
throughout? Or is it a miscellaneous collection of components,
no more integrally connected to one another than the contents
of an attic?

The first thing to be said on this score is that Christian teaching has not simply accumulated, like a snowball rolling down a
hill. Circumstances have arisen from time to time that made it
necessary for the Christian community to draw a line between
what it does and does not teach, and at the same time between

itself and other communities. That is what happened at Chalcedon in 451, and I will discuss another example in the next chapter. But these occasions have been rare. On the whole, the church has been reluctant to draw such lines, and has almost always drawn them only on very specific points and in response to very specific controversies affecting its common life.

The next thing to be said is that Christian tradition went on for a long time before its overall consistency became a major concern. Paul has been called, not inappropriately, the first Christian theologian, but he was first and foremost the bearer of a message. Whatever theology his letters contain is woven into his preaching. So it was for perhaps a thousand years more: the message of Jesus Christ went on being proclaimed and heard, handed down and interpreted in homilies, expositions, and commentaries, which were themselves copied and preserved and read. Theology was one aspect of this handing-down process rather than a distinct activity. It was practiced as a sideline, mostly by those who held administrative or pastoral offices in the church. 'Systematic' theology, the orderly and encyclopedic presentation of the whole range of Christian teaching, was virtually unknown until the middle ages.

Before the whole Christian tradition could be considered at once, it had to be assembled. Electronic data-processing has made it hard to imagine the enormous amount of humdrum labor it took to find, catalogue, translate, and arrange all the relevant texts. The first attempt was made around the year 600, but the project went on for centuries. It was still by and large a handing down of tradition, modified only in that what was handed down was sorted according to topics. Eventually, however, it began to appear that on many of these topics the traditional stock of teaching included diverse materials. There seemed to be discrepancies and even contradictions. A new task presented itself, one of finding a way to comprehend and reconcile all the various, and at first glance disparate, interpretations of what the Christian message means. The stage was set for theology to come into its own as an intellectual discipline distinct from the practice of Christian religion, engaged with questions that might or might not be directly concerned with the common life of the church.

These questions were lectured on and debated in the schools, ancestors of the modern university, from which the medieval approach to theology takes its general name: scholasticism. The work of the scholastics has almost always received mixed reviews. It is pretty much abandoned at present, and I am not interested in rehabilitating it. What cannot be gainsaid is that the best of the scholastic theologians did achieve their aim, an orderly exposition of Christian thought, comprehensive in scope and presented with a precision and depth that were the equal of any other endeavor of the mind. The treatises they produced cover all the bases, systematically and painstakingly. Dryly and didactically too, perhaps; but that is true of all schoolbooks, which is what they were. Even their formal structure often mirrors the classroom debates that were used for instructing students.

Such a debate could be launched whenever it appeared that respectable teachers had taught incompatible doctrines. A yes-or-no question was framed. Arguments were marshalled, and a case was made for each side. The merits of both cases were minutely examined and weighed. At length, the issue was decided one way or the other. Much the same pattern appears in the unit out of which many of the great compendiums were built, notably the *Summa Theologiae* of Thomas Aquinas. For reasons that I trust will become clear in due course, a brief sample of Thomas's method is useful to consider at this point.

In the third and final part of his *Summa* Thomas takes up a series of questions pertaining to Jesus Christ. He begins with the doctrine of the Incarnation, "as this means God becoming man for our salvation." In the course of this investigation, Thomas asks what kind of union the Incarnation was; more particularly, whether the union of the Word of God with human flesh took place in a 'nature.' That is the question. Having posed it, he

considers the arguments *pro* and *con*. To begin with, there seems
to be reason to believe that the union did take place in a nature.
One prominent teacher of the early church said explicitly that it
did, and two others, as well as one of the creeds used in Christian
worship, seem to imply the same thing. On the other hand, however, there is the definition of Chalcedon. I have already quoted
its teaching on the question at issue: one and the same Christ is
to be acknowledged in *two* natures, 'without confusion, without
change, without division, without separation; the distinction of
natures in no way being annulled by the union.' From that, it
would seem to follow that the union did *not* take place in one
nature.

Thomas himself, following his usual pattern, will eventually
endorse this second side of the question, the one he presents
'on the other hand.' But he does not just take sides arbitrarily.
There appears to be a contradiction within the tradition, a yes-
or-no question. Thomas, not content to flip a coin, proceeds to
resolve it. Everything turns, he suggests, on what is meant by
'nature'—as notoriously ambiguous a word in Latin and Greek
as it is in English. For clarification, Thomas goes to the philosophy of Aristotle, whose precise definition of 'nature' he
adopts. Armed with this definition, he sorts out the three different ways in which one thing can be constituted out of two.
One kind of union results from accidental joining, as with the
stones and beams of a house; another from mixture, as with a
drop of water in a bottle of wine; and a third from composition,
as with the soul and body of a human being. But if the Incarnation belonged to any of these types of union, it would contradict
other points of Christian teaching that Thomas has already dealt
with. Logically, then, the union of divine and human in Christ
cannot have taken place in a single nature. The Chalcedonian
doctrine is therefore correct. But what becomes of the arguments
that favor the opposite view? Thomas returns to them, and shows
with Aristotle's aid that each can be interpreted in a way that is
consistent with his own answer to the question, namely that the
Incarnation did not take place in a nature.

Explicating Thomas's theology is a job for specialists. The précis I have just given cannot do justice to either the sweep of his thinking or its subtlety. For one thing, I have discussed only one of the articles in which he inquires about the kind of union the Incarnation was. There are eleven more, and together they answer only one of fifty-nine questions about Christ taken up in the third part of his *Summa*. Thomas is nothing if not thorough. Nevertheless, this small example is relevant here. Four comments will suggest why.

A first comment concerns philosophy. In order to meet the challenge of systematizing, on every topic, the Christian tradition as he had received it, Thomas enlisted outside aid. What he needed was a set of basic terms, clearly defined, logically related, and applicable to anything that could be thought about. The Christian tradition itself provided no such conceptual equipment, but the newly rediscovered works of Aristotle did, and like others among the scholastics Thomas welcomed this philosophy and adapted it for use as a framework on which to weave the many strands of Christian teaching into one great tapestry.

A second comment concerns innovation. The scholastics worked on a tradition, but in a highly untraditional way. Thomas's treatment of the Chalcedonian definition is a case in point. The definition itself was composed in order to settle a single issue, the propriety of language that was being used in Christian prayer and preaching. It declares that when Christians speak of Christ as divine and also of Christ as human, they are speaking about one and the same Christ. It does not go into other questions or attempt to settle *how* Christ can be one and the same. Thomas does. By doing it he goes beyond anything the bishops at Chalcedon envisioned.

A third comment concerns an assumption on which the whole scholastic project rests. Stated oversimply, it is that anything which is true is true always and everywhere. Knowledge of what really is so must be certain knowledge, and certainty is not

certainty if it changes. In itself, this is a philosophical position
that Aristotle espoused and elaborated. But it fits quite well with
a theological position that Thomas shared with Vincent of Lérins:
the Christian message, because it is given by God, is true always
and everywhere. Like knowledge of what is so, knowledge of what
God has revealed to be so can only be certain and unchanging
knowledge. Some important consequences follow. Thomas makes
no effort to understand the definition of Chalcedon (or any of
the other traditional doctrines he quotes) in what would today be
called its original context. There is hardly a hint in his *Summa*
that he thought of the past as remote or strange, partly because
the idea of any real change in truth, especially Christian truth,
was not one that he entertained.

A fourth comment concerns the approach that Thomas's
theology exemplifies. His aim, I have said, was to synthesize and
reconcile all of Christian doctrine. In practice, this came down to
reconciling the sources of doctrine, its *auctours*, authors, authorities. Some of these authoritative sources have a special status for
Thomas; he refers to Paul as *the* apostle, for example, and
Aristotle is *the* philosopher. But in another sense all of the authors
he quotes are on an equal footing: it is enough simply to quote
them. On a given question, *A, B,* and *C* may be cited in support
of one opinion; *D, E,* and *F* in support of the opposite. But since
all of them are authorities, they are all presumed to be stating
what is in fact so. That is why the question arose at all.

Thus particular questions of the kind scholastic theology
addressed are rooted in a more general one. Let it be granted that
Christian sources are authoritative, *that* what they teach is true.
How then is it true? What is the overall pattern of reality into
which these doctrines fit? All-embracing orderliness—that was the
vision of the medieval theologians, and it was not theirs alone.
Distinction, definition, tabulation, and synthesis were esteemed
in every department of culture. Codifying and cataloguing, organ-
izing and system-building were the order of the day. I have called
Thomas's *Summa* a tapestry. The same metaphor applies to the

vast, intricate, crowded, yet unified world of meaning in which people of the middle ages lived and especially in which they thought. There was a place for everything, and poets no less than theologians, Dante no less than Thomas, saw to it that everything was in its proper place. At the same time as theology was being sorted out and tidied up, so were ethics and the law, the arts and the sciences. And each of these in turn had a place in the tapestry.

The materials, warp and weft, came from books. Those who wove it had not only a penchant for orderly design but also a reluctance to flatly disbelieve anything that an old *auctour* had said. The authors they drew on were a very mixed lot—pagan, Jewish, and Christian; philosophers, poets, chroniclers, and theologians. Discrepancies were bound to appear. But resolving . them was part of the fun. Not that fitting everything together was a mere game, an enormous ideational jigsaw puzzle. It was fun, but it was important, serious, even awesome fun. For everything *ought* to fit together. The structure of the universe was not just orderly; it was ordained. Everyone and everything, persons as well as plants and planets, had a prescribed niche in the design. There was plenty of room within the overall pattern for activity, motion, growth and decay, but these changes were themselves orderly, like the movements of a pavane, thus reflecting the changeless order of eternity. In a word, medieval culture was normative. There was, in principle, one world, one structured society, one comprehensive set of facts, beliefs, values, and ideals. What lay beyond was not culture at all, but barbarism.

That there was, and could be, only one culture properly so called was not in itself a medieval idea. It was part of the heritage of antiquity that scholasticism sought to combine with Christianity, and it survived long after the world of the middle ages had dissolved. It is frequently referred to as the classicist view of culture. For the classicist (in this sense) there are permanent, universally valid norms and ideals. True, things do change as time goes on, but the changes have no serious significance, because *times* do not change in any fundamental way. Anything that is really important or valuable can only be, ideally if not always in fact, as it was in the beginning, is now, and ever shall be world without end. Good manners, good taste, good sense; perennial philosophy, the constancy of human nature, the wisdom of the ages, immortal works of art, imperishable literature—these endure the vicissitudes of time. To know them is to be liberally educated. To have assimilated them is to be a civilized human being.

So, to return to the point from which this section began, Vincent of Lérins was a dyed-in-the-wool classicist. So was Thomas Aquinas. So have been most Christian theologians. Scholasticism is but one example of how reflection on the meaning of the Christian message has been carried out in what Edward Farley aptly calls 'the house of authority.' The diagram on the next page will help to make the point of the metaphor.

In my floorplan each of the rooms is furnished with a doctrine. Asking a question leads through a hallway and into another room, which has the answer to the question. Starting at the top of the diagram, you might ask why Christians believe in the Incarnation. One reason is that it was revealed by God. How do they know what God has revealed? For one thing, because they believe scripture to be the divinely inspired witness to revelation. On what ground do they believe that? Among others, on the ground that the Christian community had God's guidance when it accepted certain writings as its scriptures. Why do they believe that God took a hand? Partly, because they believe that God is the kind of God who orders human affairs towards salvation. And how do they know that? Above all, because the Word of God himself became human. Thus the questioner, as Farley puts it, "has been referred from one room to another in the house of authority to find himself or herself back in the original room."

My diagram is of course a vast oversimplification, intended only to suggest the way classicist theology tends to connect Christian teachings. Not every Christian theologian, classicist or

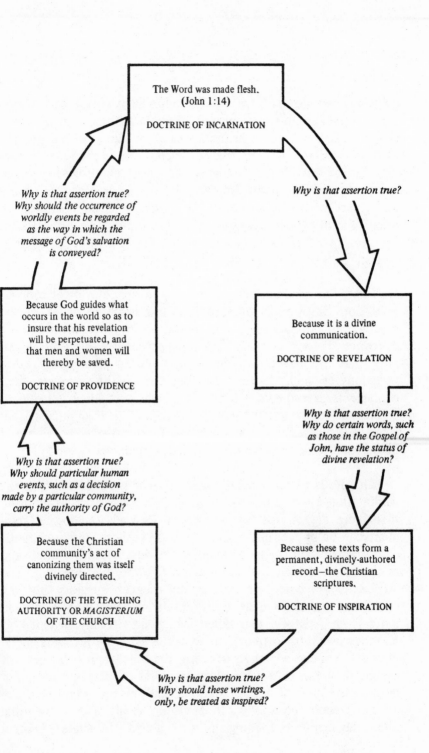

The Word was made flesh.
(John 1:14)

DOCTRINE OF INCARNATION

*Why is that assertion true?
Why should the occurrence of
worldly events be regarded
as the way in which the
message of God's salvation
is conveyed?*

Why is that assertion true?

Because God guides what
occurs in the world so as to
insure that his revelation
will be perpetuated, and
that men and women will
thereby be saved.

DOCTRINE OF PROVIDENCE

Because it is a divine
communication.

DOCTRINE OF REVELATION

*Why is that assertion true?
Why do certain words, such
as those in the Gospel of
John, have the status of
divine revelation?*

*Why is that assertion true?
Why should particular human
events, such as a decision
made by a particular community,
carry the authority of God?*

Because the Christian
community's act of
canonizing them was itself
divinely directed.

DOCTRINE OF THE TEACHING
AUTHORITY OR *MAGISTERIUM*
OF THE CHURCH

Because these texts form a
permanent, divinely-authored
record—the Christian
scriptures.

DOCTRINE OF INSPIRATION

*Why is that assertion true?
Why should these writings,
only, be treated as inspired?*

otherwise, would agree with it. There has been a lot of quarrelling, for example, about whether any such room as the one in the lower left-hand corner belongs in the house at all. Some would prefer a hallway joining the doctrine of inspiration directly with the doctrine of providence. Others would prefer an altogether different floorplan. The point, however, is not the architecture of any particular 'house of authority' but what goes on inside all of them: a kind of theological thinking that depends on authoritative sources. Two further comments on the diagram will conclude this section.

First, the general doctrines housed in the four lower rooms—revelation, inspiration of scripture, the teaching office of the church, and providence—have a logical priority over more specific doctrines. To accept these four is to accept, by implication, not only that 'the Word was made flesh' but a great many other assertions as well. Because the four (or, in other houses, their equivalents) are the foundation of all the rest, they are said to belong to 'fundamental theology.' Because they come first from a logical point of view, they are usually the first to be discussed in systematic treatments of Christian doctrine.

This leads to the second comment. The ground on which the whole 'house of authority' stands is the classicist assumption that there are eternal verities. Within its walls theological argument can be impeccably logical, because authoritative statements of Christian truth are assumed to be just as universally valid as the rules of logic that are used to regulate their meaning. The arguments are often circular, as my diagram suggests, but the circle can be as wide as reality itself. Scholasticism borrowed more from Aristotle than logic, which he virtually invented. It also borrowed basic terms. In so far as these terms were metaphysical, concerned, that is, with the unchanging essences of things, they too reflect the classicist point of view. On the other hand, metaphysical terms (like 'nature' in my example from Thomas) could be applied to anything at all, and so by using them the medieval theologians were able to integrate Christian doctrine with other fields of learning. Theirs was, at its best, a magnificent achievement. It did not last.

3

Meaning changes. The reason, to borrow a remark from Bernard Lonergan, is that while an animal with nothing to do goes to sleep, a human being with nothing to do may ask questions. Any new question alters the thinking, the knowing, and the deciding that structure the human world. A new question of fundamental importance can change that world dramatically. Scholastic theology itself was, in part, the answer to a question: how could the Christian tradition be squared with Aristotle's philosophical account of the world? And the slow collapse of scholasticism in particular and the 'house of authority' in general was bound up with another question. Frederick E. Crowe has pointed out in his *Theology of the Christian Word* that although this question had been simmering for a long time, it was the great reformer Martin Luther who first brought it to a boil.

"Holy Scriptures and the old teachers" were reappearing, Luther wrote, and as a result "people everywhere in the world begin to ask not what but why this and that was said." As I suggested in the previous section, 'why this and that was said' is the kind of question that can lead from room to room, doctrine to doctrine, within a theological 'house of authority.' Luther, however, gave it a new twist. He and the other reformers asked 'why this and that was said' because they recognized, tentatively and not always clearly, that there is more to the diversity of the Christian tradition than the scholastics had thought. What the church taught in its earliest years and what it was teaching in the sixteenth century were simply not the same. There had been a real change. And the reformers argued that the difference could not be made to vanish by what they regarded as scholasticism's philosophical sleight-of-hand. A choice had to be made: which was to be the authority for Christian doctrine, the sixteenth century or the first? Whatever the teachers of scholasticism happened to be saying, or only so much of it as could be grounded in 'Holy Scriptures and the old teachers'?

Once the matter had been put so clearly, no one could deny that a real problem existed. No one did deny it. Those who took ship with Luther and the other reformers eventually threw overboard the accretions, as they considered them, which had gathered around the Christian message since it was first proclaimed; those who did not were none the less obliged to reconsider their òwn teaching and show that it had a firm basis. The ins and outs of the ensuing debate, which splintered the Western church, are extremely intricate. It was far more than a theological debate. But in so far as it was theological, it was at bottom a debate about authority.

In that regard, Luther's significance lies in his having insisted that the truth of what the church teaches is not guaranteed simply by the fact that the church teaches it. Doctrine must be grounded. The question was, where? In a single authoritative source, said Luther's followers, that is, in scripture. In seven different sources, said a very influential treatise published at just the same time by a theologian on the opposite side of the controversy. The point I want to make is that although the answers were not the same, they were the same *kind* of answer. Both sides agreed that the question of 'why this and that was said' could be put to rest by reference to sources. In other words the Christian church, divided though it was, went on living in the 'house of authority.' Different sources were appealed to, but the appeals had a family likeness. Texts could still be used, and were used, as they had been for centuries—as quarries out of which discrete, independent, and equally valid nuggets of truth could be chiseled.

This is not to say that the sixteenth-century crisis was unimportant. It was very important, not least because the discord it fostered became, sadly, a tradition. From the standpoint of this chapter, however, its importance lay in calling attention to change, particularly change within the process of handing down Christian doctrine, so that a new set of questions was introduced into Christian theology. New answers had to wait perhaps another three hundred years; meanwhile, in the seventeenth century, another movement began.

In the frequently quoted words of the historian Herbert Butterfield, what happened then "outshines everything since the rise of Christianity and reduces the Renaissance and Reformation to the rank of mere episodes, mere internal displacements, within the system of medieval Christendom." It "changed the character of men's habitual mental operations even in the conduct of the non-material sciences." It transformed "the whole diagram of the physical universe and the very texture of human life itself." It was "the real origin both of the modern world and of the modern mentality."

It was the rise of modern science.

4

Why is the scientific revolution, as it is called, important for the topic at hand? In the previous chapter I discussed the lived world, the human world of meaning; in this one, theology as a discipline concerned with interpreting what religion has to say both about that world and to it. More particularly, I have outlined a style of theology that is very much at home within the horizon of what I have called the classicist world. When and why that world gave way to modernity has been subject to a good deal of debate, which there is no need to take part in here. Suffice it to say that Butterfield is right. On the whole, modern thinking owes more to natural science than to anything else. For the scientific revolution was not only a revolution within science. It precipitated other conflicts, among them the "warfare of science with theology."

In relation to the rest of this chapter, however, what theologians say *versus* what scientists say is less important than the
reasons both have for saying what they do. The more basic issue
is the one Luther raised—not the *what* but the *why* of Christian
doctrine. But here too Butterfield's assessment is just: new and
significant though it was, the reformers' question effected only
an 'internal displacement' within the classicist world of the middle
ages. For no matter how it was answered, the question itself was
construed as a question about the sources that ground and
authorize Christian truth; whereas the very idea that truth depends
on authoritative sources is one that the modern mentality, generally speaking, finds uncongenial. If the medieval mind typically
found it hard to disbelieve old authors, precisely because they
were old, the modern mind typically finds it hard to believe them
for the same reason. The premium it puts on novelty is one of
modernity's hallmarks. The words 'new' and 'improved' have
become Siamese twins, a kind of compound adjective that eval-
uates as it describes, blending innovation and worth into one
attribute. Conversely, what is not new is apt to be seen as out-
moded rather than venerable.

It can be argued that this characteristically modern attitude
towards antiquity was already going strong, especially in politics,
when the scientific revolution was just getting up steam. But
wherever the campaign against the past began, natural science
soon took the lead in sweeping away the old authorities, together
with the tapestry into which they had been woven. *Nullius in
verba*, 'nothing on say-so, nothing merely reported,' was the
official motto of London's Royal Society and the unofficial
motto of the whole movement. One of its most influential fore-
runners, Francis Bacon, thought that "the state of knowledge is
not prosperous nor greatly advancing, and that a way must be
opened for the human understanding entirely different from any
hitherto known." The authorities of the past must be set aside
in order that, "after the lapse of so many ages, philosophy and
the sciences may no longer float in air, but rest on the solid
foundation of experience of every kind, and the same well

examined and weighed." The kind of science Bacon envisioned was to be experimental, based not simply on observations of nature but on "nature under constraint and vexed . . . forced out of her natural state and squeezed and molded." And Bacon made it quite clear whose authority in particular this new science would replace: he named his own method after Aristotle's.

Everyone knows the stock example of how the modern approach to science overturned the Aristotelian tradition. On the basis of his metaphysical philosophy, Aristotle taught that the heavier of two bodies falls more rapidly. Galileo showed that he was wrong by dropping things from the *campanile* in Pisa and noting that they hit the ground at the same time. Now the question of just what Galileo and other early modern experimenters were up to is a good deal more complex than this, and so is the question of what Aristotle thought about falling bodies. That, in a way, is the point. The oversimplified version I have just rehearsed is the one that has entered the common fund of modern culture. It comes as a surprise that Thomas Aquinas's teacher, more than three centuries before Galileo, disproved Aristotelian science on several points, such as the eating habits of eels. But the story most people have grown up with features Galileo as a hero in the march against obscurantism, a martyr to the cause of science, whether this version is historically accurate or not.

I have already suggested two ways in which the community of modern scientists is like other communities: it is the bearer and the product of a tradition, and its work depends on belief. Outside this professional community, however (and to some extent within it) a tradition *about* science has established itself. Its tone was set when science was young:

> *Nature and Nature's laws lay hid in night:*
> *God said, Let Newton be! and all was light.*

Alexander Pope's couplet puts the science of mechanics at the beginning of a sacred saga, a new Genesis. When he wrote it, the

human world was still understood in religious terms. Theology
was still a background for posing the great questions of where
we come from, where we are going, how we get there. But it was
a fading background. As science painted a new one, God was
left out of the picture. Stephen Toulmin, philosopher and historian of science, makes the perceptive comment that the collected sermons with which educated people in the eighteenth
century stocked their libraries have a modern counterpart, in that
"the popular scientist has won over the audience of the popular
preacher."

How much of what popular scientists preach is science,
though, is a very good question. 'Scientism' has been defined as
science out of bounds, but the boundaries are not always easy to
determine. The views expressed by those who talk about rela-
tivity are not necessarily those of Einstein. The idea of a 'running-
down universe' may or may not be an accurate interpretation of
the laws of thermodynamics. In everyday conversation 'evolution'
is used in a way that goes beyond what biologists, as biologists,
would endorse. The very word 'science' has significant overtones.
When Bertrand Russell laid it down that 'what science cannot tell
us, mankind cannot know,' his pronouncement, strictly speaking,
was a tautology. That science is what we know is true by definition. In that sense, heraldry and homemaking are sciences,
branches of knowledge, just as much as botany and bacteriology.
Russell might just as well have said that what cannot be known
cannot be known.

That is not what he meant, of course. He was using 'science'
in the modern sense, which limits it to one particular kind of
knowing. In that sense, 'what science cannot tell us' is equivalent
to 'what cannot be understood by using the methods that have
produced such notable results in mechanics, physics, chemistry,
and the like.' Stated positively, any knowledge worthy of the
name has got to be the result of such procedures. Unfortunately,
just what those procedures might be is up for debate, and the
question is made all the more complicated by the fact that what

scientists actually do, as Einstein himself observed, is not necessarily the same as what they *say* they do—not to mention what popular scientists say.

It is the commonly accepted view, however, that is important here, not because it is correct or incorrect but because it is common. In this view science is understood, in much the same way Bacon understood it, as experience well examined and weighed, where by 'experience' is meant *sense* experience and the examining is done with a battery of optical instruments and measuring devices. Accordingly, Russell's squib implies that the scope of reality, known and knowable, is the same as the scope of measurable experience. In other words, whatever is real is sensible, at least in principle. If there happens to exist any non-empirical reality, we simply do not and cannot know it. It might as well not exist.

That is why God is painted out of the scientific picture. According to traditional Christian doctrine, that reality which is most real is utterly non-empirical. God is 'without body, parts, or passions,' not extended in space or time, not an object of sense experience. It follows that *if* natural science lends support to the doctrine of empirical reality as all the reality there is, then natural science undermines the doctrine of God and the rest of Christian teaching with it. But note the *if*. I have stressed it because saying that natural science deals with empirical realities is one thing, and saying that everything real is empirical (and therefore knowable by the methods of natural science) is something else. The latter is not in itself a scientific statement at all; it is a philosophical, indeed metaphysical doctrine. Carl Sagan, I submit, was not speaking as a scientist when he opened his televised exploration by announcing, "The cosmos is all that is or ever was or ever will be."

He was, however, stating a view that is very much a part of modernity. The same great questions about where we come from, where we are going, and how we get there are still being asked. Now the answers are framed, more likely than not, in para-scientific terms. In the beginning, the Big Bang; in the end, a state of maximum randomness; in the meantime, computers and genetic engineering. Somewhat ironically, a world of meaning has been constructed on the authority of a tradition that began by rejecting traditional authority.

There is no need to dwell on how enormously modern science has changed the very texture of human life. The change goes on and may be expected to continue, as may the debate over whether it has uniformly been a change for the better. But even if 'new' is not always synonymous with 'improved'; even if much was lost in the transition from classicism to modernity; even if nature, 'forced out of her natural state and squeezed and molded,' has a way of being uninhabitable, there is no going back. The human life whose texture science has changed now depends on science for its survival. How then has Christianity responded to the change?

At the beginning of this section I suggested that the real impact of natural science on theology has been deeper and less direct than particular battles of the Genesis-or-geology sort. It was said by T.H. Huxley, who took the bishop to task in a famous debate about evolution, that extinguished theologians lie about the cradle of every science like the snakes strangled by the infant Hercules. Possibly he exaggerated. Anyhow he missed the point. Butterfield comes closer in the passage quoted above, when he points out that natural science 'changed the character of men's habitual mental operations even in the conduct of the non-material sciences.'

The change was important, first of all, because it occurred. The fact that it did occur undid classicism's cardinal tenet, the assumption that the character of mental operations is part of human nature and therefore does not change. But if mental operations can change, so can everything those operations construct--not only the natural sciences, but also communities, laws, institutions, language, literature, art, even culture as a whole. That being so, culture could no longer be conceived as normative. It too would have to be studied empirically, in the sense that there are different cultures, different worlds 'thrown together' by different symbols, different styles of thinking and different ways of life. And from that it would follow that the disciplines which study the human world of meaning, what Butterfield calls the 'non-empirical sciences,' must undergo a revolution no less sweeping than the one in the sciences that study the world of nature.

Such a revolution did take place. The nineteenth century saw a change in the character of the mental operations performed by scholars. They became aware of *history*. Whereas classicism thought of itself as perennial and normative, modern historical scholarship began to recognize that times change. Whereas classicism stressed eternal verities and the ideal of certainty, historians began to stress the ties that bind ideas to particular eras and ages. Most importantly, whereas classicism tended to take old authors at their word, modern scholars began to adopt critical methods for probing beneath what was said to learn what had been meant by saying it.

It is not hard to see how all of this leads to a way of understanding the sources of Christian doctrine far different from the way they are understood in the 'house of authority.' Classicist theology marshalls quotations from authoritative texts, on the assumption that they mean what they have always meant and always will; historical scholarship inquires about their original surroundings, on the assumption that meaning changes. Classicism interpreted the Christian tradition in what it took to be a timeless framework of logic; modern scholarship interprets that framework itself in the larger context of history. Coping with the effects of the nineteenth-century revolution in the non-material sciences has been, and still is, the central issue in modern theology. But the questions it involves are too important for the end of a chapter. They need one of their own.

❧ FIVE ❧
Doctrines and History

It is very meete, righte, and oure bounden duetie, that we should at al tymes, and in al places, geue thankes to thee O Lorde, almightye euerlasting God, which art one God, one Lorde, not one onely person, but three persones in one substaunce: For that which we beleue of the glory of the father, the same we beleue of the sōne, and of the holy ghost, without any difference, or inequalitie . . .

THE BOOK OF COMMON PRAYER, 1549

THIS CHAPTER TAKES its bearings from three directions: detective stories, a comment made in a letter to the Roman emperor Trajan, and a bit of juvenile banter. A miscellaneous lot, these; none of them, on the face of it, bears much relation to doctrines, and only the second to history. By now, however, I expect the reader will have become accustomed to my somewhat sidelong way of approaching the topic at hand. In any case the three paths I propose to follow do, at length, converge.

First, detective stories. I begin with them because anyone who follows the unravelling of a classic whodunnit mystery is getting at least a glimpse of the sort of thing modern historians do. Not that the detection of criminals and the writing of history are identical; there are important differences between them, as well as similarities. Yet both are exercises in reconstructing the past, and in that respect their similarities are many and strong enough to have prompted the historian and philosopher R.G. Collingwood to compose his own miniature tale of detection in order to illustrate the sort of reasoning historical scholars use as they go about their work.

Collingwood begins with the obligatory corpse in the library. On the dagger with which the deceased, one John Doe, had obviously been stabbed, there was a smear of green paint. That very afternoon Doe himself had put a coat of exactly the same paint on the gate that stood between his house and the rectory next door. The local police had already listened to an accusation and a confession (both of which they dismissed as preposterous) when the rector's daughter arrived to tell them that hers was the hand that had wielded the dagger. The only effect of this second confession, · however, was to draw official attention to three facts: first, her current beau, Richard Roe by name, was a medical student (and would thus know all the most effective places to stab); second, Roe had spent the night in the rectory next door to John Doe's house; third, when the dampness of his shoes was remarked, Roe admitted that he had gone outdoors during a brief but heavy rain, about midnight, but would not say why.

To these clues were added what Detective-Inspector Jenkins of Scotland Yard found in the rectory dustbin: the ashes of what had probably been a pair of gloves and a lot of writing paper, together with some metal buttons stamped with the name of a well-known glove maker whose wares the rector was known to favor. As Jenkins's investigation proceeded, it became known that on the day after John Doe's death the rector had donated one of his jackets to a certain needy parishioner. This jacket proved upon examination to be quite shapeless, as though it had recently been soaked in water, and on the right cuff there was more of Doe's green paint.

Such are the clues. The first thing to note is that by themselves they add up to nothing more than a list of unconnected facts. It is up to Jenkins to fit them into an intelligible pattern. His job is to reconstruct what happened, by constructing a narrative that accounts for all the relevant evidence, and this he eventually does. His hypothetical account begins with certain letters which proved that the rector's wife, now dead, had many years ago indulged in an affair resulting in the birth of the rector's supposed daughter.

These letters were in John Doe's possession, and he had long been using them to blackmail the rector. Shortly before his violent death Doe sent a further demand for money—one too many. The rector decided to make use of his familiarity with the neighboring Doe house for the purpose of eliminating its occupant. As he left the rectory, wearing gloves, his furtive manner was observed by his guest Richard Roe. Becoming suspicious, Roe followed. The storm broke. But the rector worked quickly, and succeeded in ending Doe's blackmail by ending his life.

The virtue of this narrative is that it brings all the evidence into a coherent pattern. It explains why green paint was found where it was (it was dark when the rector opened the freshly-painted gate), why letters were burned (they were the proof of his wife's escapade), why the rector's jacket and Roe's shoes had been soaked (both men had been out in the midnight storm), why the rector got rid of the jacket and destroyed his gloves (he had noticed the paint on them), why Richard Roe refused to give a reason for his having been out in the downpour (he wanted to conceal the suspicious movements of his sweetheart's father), and why the rector's daughter had confessed (she suspected Roe of having committed the murder, on account of his shoes and his reticence, and wanted to distract attention from him). Rather a convincing case, taking it all together. True, the same facts might have been susceptible of a different interpretation. But Collingwood ends his tale in the classical manner, with a *denouement* that clinches the case. By dropping some well-placed hints as to the shape his hypothesis was taking, Detective-Inspector Jenkins gets a decisive confirmation: the rector, preferring not to be hanged, commits suicide.

Such a tidy ending is seldom possible in the kind of investigation historians pursue. That is perhaps the most important way their work differs from the investigations of detective fiction. Apart from this, the case of John Doe exhibits much the same sort of procedure used in historical scholarship. The first point to be made about the narrative of what happened before and after the murder is that the data or clues—the paint, the ashes, and so on—are not just pieced together in scissors-and-paste fashion. They are accounted for by a construction of the investigator's imagination. A second point is that what accounts for each piece of evidence is a deliberate human action. All of the characters do what they do for their own reasons. In light of what they knew about the situation, what they inferred from their knowledge, and what they wanted to happen, each of them made certain decisions and acted on them. The rector's daughter, for example, knew that John Doe had been killed, that it had rained heavily at just about the time of the murder, that her admirer Richard Roe had got his shoes wet the same night, and that he declined to state why he had left the rectory at just the crucial time. She concluded from all of this that he was the murderer, she thought it likely that the detective from Scotland Yard would presently reach the same conclusion, she hoped that a red herring might still be drawn across his path, and she decided to claim that she herself had stabbed Doe. Knowing, drawing conclusions, judging probability, hoping, and deciding—the result of these conscious acts was one of the pieces of evidence that Jenkins had to account for, namely, the rector's daughter's confession.

This leads to a third point. The detective does not take her confession at face value. Rather, as Collingwood puts it, "he begins attending seriously to this statement at the point where he stops treating it as a statement, that is, as a true or false account of her having done the murder, and begins treating the fact that she makes it as a fact which may be of service to him." The question he has to ask is what the statement means. But that is not, in the first instance, a question as to what the statement is *about*, namely the identity of the murderer. It is a question about the rector's daughter. Why is she making this statement? Because it is true; because she did in fact kill John Doe? That is one possible answer—but only one, and in this case the wrong one. She might also be making it out of sheer vanity, or fear, or expediency, or a desire to call attention to herself, or—as turned out to be correct—a desire to protect someone else.

This third point is quite central. Modern historians, like Collingwood's detective, are critical. They distinguish between a statement as statement on one hand, and the same statement as evidence on the other; they ask what it is evidence for; they determine how far and in what way they will use the statement, as evidence, to reconstruct what happened. And their adoption of critical methods is the main thing (though not the only one) that distinguishes modern historians from their predecessors. It is not that historians did not exist before modern times. They did. Nor were these earlier historians oblivious to the existence of forgeries and falsehoods among the statements on which they based their narratives of the past. For example, when John Milton, one of the last of this older breed, wrote his *History of Britain* he knew that he had only legends to draw on for an account of England in pre-Roman times. But, he comments in his first chapter, "that which hath receav'd approbation from so many, I have chosen not to omitt." As for the question of accuracy, "be that upon the credit of those whom I must follow"–not on Milton himself. His job, as he sees it, is to pass on what has been "attested by ancient Writers from Books more ancient"; that is "the due and proper subject of Story."

Milton's is a classicist view of the historian's craft. He is not altogether uncritical. But he is, for the most part, content to take the statements of the old authors at face value, *as* statements rather than as evidence. And it is significant in this regard that he refers to what he is writing as 'story.' In the seventeenth century this word was still more or less synonymous with 'history'; either of them could be used for most kinds of narrative about the past. Thus writing the history of Britain was, for Milton, telling the story of Britain. It was transmitting a heritage that had received, and presumably would continue to receive, the 'approbation of many.' This is not to say that his readers, like Tolkien's hobbits, preferred to read books that told them what they already knew. They were, however, people whose corporate story was the story Milton set out to tell. His book is not an exhortation to patriotism, in the way some of Shakespeare's historical plays are, but neither is it the kind of dispassionate monograph that modern scholars publish.

The point at present is that narrating the past can serve different purposes, that clear distinctions between them were only beginning to be drawn when Milton wrote, and that only one of them is the concern of today's critical historians. H. Richard Niebuhr illustrates one important distinction by juxtaposing two accounts of the same event. The first is Abraham Lincoln's:

> Four-score and seven years ago our fathers brought forth upon this continent a new nation, conceived in liberty and dedicated to the proposition that all men are created equal.

The second account appears in the *Cambridge Modern History*:

> On July 4, 1776, Congress passed the resolution which made the colonies independent communities, issuing at the same time the well-known Declaration of Independence. If we regard the Declaration as the assertion of an abstract political theory, criticism and condemnation are easy. It sets out with a general proposition so vague as to be practically useless.

Lincoln was telling the American story. In fact his Gettysburg Address has become part of that story, taking its place with the Boston Tea Party, Betsy Ross and her flag, the westward trek of the covered wagons, and so on. Recounting such a story can fire the imagination, root the present in a noble past, promote community spirit, instil ideals, inspire commitment, and launch the future. And there is no reason why this kind of evaluative history should not be written. The purpose for which critical historians write, however, is different.

Historians are of course human beings. As such they are more or less patriotic, more or less committed to and motivated by values and causes; they have more or less definite convictions about what is worthy and admirable. But as historians—as members of a community of specialists in a scholarly discipline—

it is not their primary job to propose policies or promote action. Their aim as scholars is to organize the evidence of the past, to understand what was occurring, and to establish historical facts in so far as they can be established. Those facts may well have a bearing on the present and on the future. If so, the historian may, indirectly, further some social or cultural or religious goal by reconstructing social, cultural, or religious events. But that is not the principal reason for taking up historical scholarship.

Lest this last remark be misunderstood, I would stress that I am not subscribing to what Bernard Lonergan calls 'the principle of the empty head,' which demands that before you attempt to understand historical evidence you must forget everything you have been told, bracket everyone else's interpretation, unload the baggage of the past, assume a neutral position, judge the case solely on its merits, and generally let the facts speak for themselves. This seemingly reasonable advice has two things against it. In the first place, the claim that scholarly work must begin by eliminating prior judgments is itself a prior judgment, to the effect that prior judgments are always bad. But in the second place, and more importantly, facts simply do not speak. In Collingwood's miniature mystery, for example, Richard Roe's shoes are soggy. That is a fact. Whether it 'says' anything, whether it is a significant fact, whether the condition of Roe's shoes is related to anything else, is not a fact but a question, and someone had to ask it. How did they *get* wet? How *do* shoes get wet? Who had been wearing them, and when? What about the cloudburst last night? And so on. The example is not very profound, but its point is general: how historical evidence is understood depends on the inquiring intelligence of the investigator. Wondering, as Aristotle said, is the beginning of every investigation, and wonder is not neutrality. An empty head asks no questions. It is quite true that if you approach the evidence having made up your mind in advance you are likely to overlook everything except what you are looking for. But at least you will find something, and what you find may prompt you to look for something new, whereas if you look for nothing in particular you will find—nothing in particular.

The neutral observer is a mythical animal. The myth begins with the idea that historical scholarship ought to be as much like natural science as possible. But historians, having tried that route and found a dead end, have come to realize that there is a fundamental difference between the data that are pertinent to their inquiries, and the data pertinent to natural science. Scholarly investigation deals with expressions of human meaning, the results of thinking, deciding, and loving. Natural-scientific investigation does not. To a large extent scientists can therefore distance themselves, as persons, from what they are investigating. Chemists do not 'identify with' potassium chlorate, physicists are not attracted to or repelled by the morality of quarks and quasars, and the relation between a botanist and a buttercup, whatever else it may be, is not an interpersonal encounter.

The historians' situation is quite different. They encounter the past by encountering, indirectly, the persons for whose thoughts and actions there is evidence in documents, artifacts, and monuments. Such things as earthquakes and eclipses are, to be sure, events that have taken place in the past. But they are *historical* events only in so far as they have had to do with human affairs. If the eruption of Mount Vesuvius had not buried Pompeii, it might interest geologists, but not historians. The events that historians endeavor to understand are things done and said by men and women—their communities, institutions, and civilizations, their ways and their words. For just that reason, only men and women can reconstruct these constructions. This calls for a further comment.

Historians are human. Each of them lives in what I have called a world of meaning. The horizon of that world will not be the same as that of a thirteenth-century Italian, say, or a first-century Christian; if it were, there would be no need for historical scholarship. The business of scholars is to enter some other time or place or both, by reassembling it from the available evidence. In so doing, they do not—they cannot—empty their heads so as to cancel the effects of their own socialization and acculturation.

That would be cancelling themselves; the result could only be something like the complete amnesia described at the beginning of chapter three. Rather, historians expand their own horizons to include the horizon of other persons. What they do is not essentially different from coming to understand how any stranger lives and thinks and loves, except that conversation *tête-à-tête* is impossible. Collingwood gives a useful example in his autobiography. He recalls how he had sat, as a boy, reading in his father's study about the battle of Trafalgar and Nelson's refusal to remove his military decorations. 'In honor I won them,' Nelson is reported to have said; 'in honor I will die with them.' Collingwood observes on one hand that unless he had been capable of thinking himself into something of the same position—decked out in medals that made an easy target for the enemy's musketeers, and asking whether this was the time to take them off for safety's sake—Nelson's words would have remained meaningless. On the other hand, no matter how vividly he imagined that distant situation, Collingwood never left his own. He was still a little boy in a jersey, and around him was the carpet of the study, not the Atlantic Ocean.

Today the process that Collingwood describes is referred to as the merging of horizons, one of which is the scholar's own. It is a long, slow, and enormously complicated process, and it cannot be boiled down to a few rules of thumb. One thing is clear, however. Any would-be scholar will have to heed that most ancient of philosophical precepts, *know thyself*. In order to understand a piece of historical evidence, a text for example, you have to understand the words, what they are about, and who it was that wrote them. But you also have to understand who you, the interpreter of the text, are. Applied to the work of historical scholarship, *know thyself* is an injunction to know your own biases, blocks, and slant on things; to know what you find repulsive, what you esteem; and, especially, to know what you do *not* know, what is no part of your world, what therefore you would overlook or misunderstand.

Discovering yourself in this sense is not a matter of solitary introspection. It depends on conversation with others, including those whose words are conveyed by writing. Encountering other people by reconstructing their thoughts and deeds can bring your own presuppositions to light just as effectively as encountering them face to face. Either way, you can discover who you are, and what your horizon is, in relation to other, perhaps strange worlds. Not that such a self-discovery is inevitable. While the strangeness of someone else's ideas and affections can, potentially, enlarge your own world of meaning and value, it can also be a barrier to understanding. I once read in a concert program, for example, that Bach's *Christmas Oratorio* expresses in music the joy that everyone feels at the birth of a child. Since nothing more was said, it would seem that whoever wrote the program notes had nothing more to say—and that he or she had therefore missed something important. Certainly the *Christmas Oratorio* is joyous, and certainly any baby is something to celebrate. But can we really understand what Bach was up to, without at least taking one rather special baby into account? I leave it as a question. But I suspect that it simply did not enter this writer's head that religious belief can motivate great music. Or, more likely, such a possibility did occur, only to be dismissed. Unwilling, or unable, to reconstruct in religious terms the construction of the human spirit that is the *Christmas Oratorio*, the writer accounted for its existence in the only way he or she knew how—Bach 'must' have been doing something else, something besides giving voice to convictions about the meaning of a certain human life that began at Bethlehem.

I have used as an example an instance of religious, and specifically Christian, meaning to make a point that applies everywhere. As a scholastic maxim puts it, whatever is received is received after the manner of the receiver. What you can comprehend, that is, depends on what you are *like*, what you have an affinity for, what fits into the world you have inherited and are making for yourself. A more familiar phrase says the same thing: it takes one to know one. If you assume that nothing is ever done except for the sake of what the doer gets out of it, you will look for that kind of motivation in what purports to be altruistic action. If you have felt no flicker of pure curiosity, no desire to find out, just for the sake of the finding, why something is so; if you have no notion that knowledge can be pursued as an end in itself, then you will be likely to ascribe all the labors of scientists and scholars to something else, economic necessity perhaps. If you suppose that in the last analysis all loving is either a manifestation of sexual libido or a substitute for it, quite a lot of poetry will be a closed book.

It has been said that all of us, by the time we reach our fortieth year, have the faces we deserve. Perhaps we do. Anyhow we all have the worlds we deserve. Finally, no one else is responsible for our outlook, convictions, and attitudes. Consequently, what you make of someone else, indeed everyone else, depends on what you have made of yourself. That on one hand. On the other, as I have already suggested, your encounter with different persons and a different world of meaning can shake or expand your own. There are perhaps no attitudes so deeply ingrained as to be beyond change, no world view so inflexible as to admit of no stretching.

And no heart so cold that it cannot be warmed. Conversion happens. That is why I put the chapter on faith at the beginning. The 'faith that is activated by love' (Gal 5:6) puts everything in a new light. It changes what is received, because it changes the receiver. Knowing yourself becomes something altogether different, because you have a new self to know. And it is this new world, the world transformed by grace, in which alone the religious doctrines that you receive from the past can make sense.

I am anticipating, though. I began this section with a detective story in order to underscore the scholarly distinction between statements as statements and as evidence. What can now be added is that what a statement is understood to be evidence *for* depends on who is doing the understanding. In order for Collingwood's Inspector Jenkins to conclude that the confession volunteered by the rector's daughter was evidence, not for who stabbed John Doe, but for her own attempt to protect Richard Roe, Jenkins had to entertain both possibilities. Had he been unable even to imagine a respectable rector's daughter deliberately misleading an officer of the law, his reconstruction of the crime would have proceeded on very different lines. As it was, he exercised a talent that G.K. Chesterton's more famous detective, Father Brown, specializes in. What this otherwise unlikely sleuth has to say about his method may suitably conclude this section. After much coaxing, Father Brown agrees to divulge the secret of his many successful cases:

> 'I had murdered them all myself,' explained Father Brown patiently. 'So, of course, I knew how it was done. . . . I had thought out exactly how a thing like that could be done, and in what style or state of mind a man could really do it. And when I was quite sure that I felt exactly like the murderer myself, of course I knew who he was. . . . I don't try to get outside the man. I try to get inside the murderer . . . thinking his thoughts, wrestling with his passions; till I have bent myself into the posture of his hunched and peering hatred . . . Till I really am a murderer.'

Here a certain amount of Chestertonian rhetoric has to be allowed for. To speak of 'becoming' a murderer, or a monarch, a Mesopotamian, or what have you, is to exaggerate. Historians do not reproduce what has been constructed in the past. They reconstruct it. But the exaggeration is on the right side. Though not himself a criminal, Father Brown could think like one. Though gentle, he knew the urge to violence. Though virtuous, he could understand vice.

So it is with historians. As persons of good will, they can apprehend what motivates human folly and wickedness, as sighted people can apprehend what it is to be blind, and apprehend it more readily than the foolish and the wicked can. The reverse, however, does not hold. It has been said that "biography should be written by an acute enemy," but on the contrary it is an acute friend who has the most acute discernment. I have already said that the business of historians is to understand the past, not to pass judgment on it. Yet it is inevitable that the way a given historian interprets human actions will reveal quite a lot about the kind of person the historian is—if not to the historian, certainly to others. A biography discloses the personality of the biographer as well as that of its subject; similarly, written history reveals both sides of a historian's encounter with the past.

2

I turn now to the second point of reference mentioned at the beginning of this chapter, a letter written to the emperor Trajan around the year 112. The writer, Pliny, had recently been sent out to reorganize one of the Asian provinces of the Roman empire. On his arrival, he reports to Trajan, he found that charges were being pressed against the members of a certain religious sect. Pliny had as yet had no dealings with these Christians, as they called themselves, and in order to get to the bottom of the accusations against them, he called in some former members of the sect for interrogation as to what went on at its secret meetings. Not much, it seems. According to Pliny's letter, these lapsed Christians "maintained that the amount of their fault or error had been this: it was their custom to assemble on a fixed day before daylight and take turns singing a hymn to Christ as a god." The report goes on to list other Christian practices, in a way which suggests that Pliny had expected to find something more lurid and loathsome. But even the third-degree methods he used on some Christian women extracted only "extravagant superstition."

The letter is important in several ways. It is one of the very few pieces of evidence for early Christian worship, all the more interesting in that it comes from an outsider. The only reprehensible thing Pliny discovered in the Christians' behavior was their refusal to take part in the official ceremony, half religious and half patriotic, of burning incense before the statues of the authorized Roman deities. And his only indication of what he meant by extravagant superstition is the line, already quoted, about the Christians' own worship. Here Pliny's Latin is not perfectly clear; he may have been telling Trajan that the Christians 'recited a form of words' at their early morning meetings, rather than 'sang a hymn.' Either way, though, their antiphonal chant was directed 'to Christ as a god.' That in itself would not have been remarkable to an early second-century Roman. Pliny's was quite a pluralistic society where religious practice was concerned. There were any number of cults, any number of gods and demigods to worship. As for paying divine honor to a man, even that was nothing out of the way. Worshipping the emperor was common enough, at least in the provinces. In fact, the extravagance of the Christians consisted in their refusing to do just that. It was their exclusiveness that was odd. If a hymn to Christ, why not incense to the emperor—especially since it was a capital offense to refuse?

Yet they did refuse, and took the consequences. It may be that the numbers and courage of the noble army of martyrs have been exaggerated somewhat; martyrdom is always excellent publicity, as the Roman officials eventually figured out. Be that as it may, two things seem clear about the early Christian communities. Explicitly, they bestowed their worship and reverence on Christ. Implicitly, they regarded any other worship as false and wicked, and declined to have anything further to do with any member who gave in when civil authority demanded a demonstration of loyalty to the emperor in the shape of participation in the official rites. Both individual Christians and their community were constituted in part by worship—not worship in general, but worship of 'Christ as a god.' To revere the emperor in the same way was to deny what the church meant and what it was.

But were these Christians not believers in one God and only one? They were. Their community was born in the synagogue, and they sided with the Jewish community in condemning as mere idols all but the God who brought Israel out of Egypt. How then could the church worship Christ too? That is an excellent question—a theological question, a very difficult question, and a question that went for something like three hundred years without a clear, precise, satisfactory answer.

It is a theological question in the sense discussed in chapter four; a question, that is, about what the language of Christian formation means, and therefore about the meaning of the gospel on which it is built. It is a difficult question, because the transformation for which that formation and that language exist is so complete and so important that mere words are always pale by comparison. The question took three centuries to ask and answer, because for the most part the church had other things to do. If it was going to transform the world, it had in the first place to stay alive. Besides sporadic persecution by the Roman government, however, there were verbal attacks to be dealt with, and so Christ was debated and discussed as well as proclaimed. But the language of worship remained primary. Who is Christ?

> *His state was divine,*
> *yet he did not cling*
> *to his equality with God*
> *but emptied himself*
> *to assume the condition of a slave,*
> *and became as men are;*
> *and being as all men are,*
> *he was humbler yet,*
> *even to accepting death,*
> *death on a cross.*
> *But God raised him high*
> *and gave him the name*
> *which is above all other names*
> *so that all beings*
> *in the heavens, on earth and in the underworld,*
> *should bend the knee at the name of Jesus*
> *and that every tongue should acclaim*
> *Jesus Christ as Lord,*
> *to the glory of God the Father* (Phil 2:6-11).

That, or something like it, may have been the hymn sung by the Christians in Pliny's province. Christ the redeemer, the source and content of the church's saving story, is in some sense divine:

this, it seems, was enough and more than enough to go by until, some two hundred years after Pliny sent his letter, a crisis erupted that could only be resolved by deciding in just *what* sense Christ is divine.

Arius, the man who precipitated this crisis, has been somewhat maligned. He was not the cold, crafty, and nearly pagan logician he is sometimes said to have been. He and those who followed his teaching were sincerely concerned about salvation, which, they asserted unequivocally, only Christ mediates. But the way they understood the mediator was of necessity part and parcel of the way they conceived his transforming effect on men and women. They called him 'Son of God,' as the church had done time out of mind, but they understood this title, and the church's other state-ments about Christ, in a way that set off an explosion. For the Arians, Jesus *became* the Son of God. He took hold of God's will for the world and unfailingly obeyed it, so that divine sonship was something he grew into, a reward given to him as God's faith-ful servant, something different in degree but not in kind from the status of Christians, God's other sons and daughters by adoption. The Arians' Christ is the firstborn, the representative, the standard to which Christians aspire—and only that. He is godly, godlike, 'as God'—but not God.

For when it came to talking about God, Arius was quite clear-headed, especially as regards the distinction between God and everything else. Arius accepted what was, by the beginning of the fourth century, the whole church's belief: there is one God, who alone is the Creator, the source of all that is, seen and unseen. God has no beginning, no source or origin. The created order does, because God has brought it into existence *ex nihilo*, out of noth-ing else at all. This utter contrast is part of what it means to say that God is God. But Christ does have a beginning. True, the church taught that "all things were made through him, and with-out him was not anything made that was made" (Jn 1:3). Equally, however, it proclaimed that he is the Son *of* God; that he is 'begotten,' generated, brought to be. Now if Christ is begotten, he has a beginning and therefore—Arius was, among other things, a logician—he is not God. And since there exist only God on one hand and creatures on the other, it follows that Christ is a creature.

Such was Arius's doctrine. He had much more to say, but the controversy centered on his contention that Christ belongs to the universe of created beings, that he had a beginning, that 'there was when he was not.' None of this appeared like a bolt from the blue; it was more like the particle of dust around which a snowflake crystallizes. As long as the Christian message had been preached there were Christians who, having made it their own, went on to ask how they might better understand it. Various ways of explaining who Christ is were tried, some of them more helpful than others. The experiments of two earlier writers deserve attention here for the light their understanding of Christ sheds on Arius's later view.

The first is Tertullian. In order to expound Christ's divinity, that is, his relation to God the Father, Tertullian makes use of several comparisons. On one or two occasions he says that the Father and the Son are 'of one substance,' which on the face of it asserts that Christ the Son of God is thoroughly divine. In fact it does not. For it is also clear that by substance Tertullian meant 'stuff,' the perceptible material God is composed of. As Son of God, Christ is a kind of extrusion of this divine stuff, almost like toothpaste from a tube. In Tertullian's opinion, "the Father is the whole substance, whereas the Son is something derived from it, and a part of it." Tertullian *asserted* that the Son is divine, but he contradicted himself by holding as well that the Son is not the whole divine substance. Nor is he eternal, as the Father is. His extrusion took place in time. For Tertullian, as later for Arius, there was once a moment when "there was no Son to make God a Father."

Tertullian's inconsistency arises out of his propensity for thinking in pictures. He held that God's substance, though of course invisible, is nevertheless material. The second writer I will consider, Origen, who died thirty years afer the death of Tertullian and shortly after the birth of Arius, had no such attachment to imagery. He insisted over and over that no material analogy applies to God, who has no bodily characteristics at all. Like Tertullian, he recognized that the church's teaching about Christ raised a real difficulty for many Christians. On one hand, he writes, they are "fearful of saying that there are two gods," and rightly so. But in order to avoid this they are liable, on the other hand, to fall back on one of two different but equally unacceptable alternatives: "either denying that the Son is really distinct from the Father . . . or else denying the Son's divinity." How can all three mistakes be avoided? That had been Tertullian's problem. Origen, however, weighed the kind of answer Tertullian gave and found it wanting. It simply will not do, in Origen's estimation, to think "that a part of God's substance was changed into the Son, or that the Son was begotten by the Father out of no substance at all, that is, from some thing external to God's own substance, so that there was a time when the Son did not exist." Origen himself has a different solution: "setting aside all thought of a material body," he argues that Christ, the Word and Wisdom of God, "was begotten of the invisible and incorporeal God apart from any bodily feeling, like an act of will proceeding from the mind."

The important thing here is Origen's use of an entirely non-material comparison: as thinking gives rise to decision in human consciousness, so the Father begets the Son. This psychological analogy in turn allowed Origen to affirm what Tertullian, because of his picture-thinking, could not, namely that the Son is in the strictest sense eternal. In that respect, he is divine—but not in all respects. Origen also held that only the Father is God pure and simple. The Son is God only 'by participation.' He is incomparably more excellent than other beings, yet there is just as great a gap between him and the Father. Origen's Christ belongs to an intermediate zone, not quite divine yet not quite creaturely either.

It was this in-between status that Arius eliminated. Whereas Origen had borrowed his notion of participation from a Greek philosopher, Arius kept to a Christian vocabulary and argued solely in terms of creatures and their Creator. Christ had to be one or the other. Which? The rest I have discussed already. Once the question 'Who is Christ?' had been posed in this new and clear-cut way, it had to be answered, and none of the earlier answers would do. Origen had been able to remedy to some extent the internal contradiction of views like Tertullian's, yet his own position was still not entirely consistent. Arius's was. That partly accounts for its popularity. The poem Arius composed for his followers could be heard far from his hometown in Egypt when the controversy began. In 325 a council of bishops was convened to resolve it.

They met at Nicea, where the emperor Constantine, a recent convert (of sorts) to Christianity, had his summer palace. The results of their deliberations were an unqualified rejection of Arianism and a corresponding statement of Christian belief. Similar creeds were already in use, but this one became standard. The full version produced at the council of Nicea is given in the appendix of this book; with a few additions and emendations, made about fifty years later, it is still recited Sunday by Sunday in Christian worship. It declares that the Lord Jesus Christ, the Son of God, is not just 'from God' but 'God from God'; that although he is indeed begotten he is 'begotten *not* made,' that is, not a creature; and that he is 'consubstantial' or 'of one substance' or, in a new translation for use in worship, 'of one Being' with the Father.

Of these assertions the last was, and is, the most significant. By no stretch of reasoning could it be understood in a sense compatible with Arianism, and it was for that reason adopted at Nicea. Not without misgivings. 'Consubstantial,' *homoousios* in Greek, was an innovation. It added a new and rather technical item to the Christian vocabulary, and moreover it smacked of pagan philosophy—two things that Arius had scrupulously avoided—and on both counts it was objected to, both at the council and afterwards, even by those who would not have dreamed of supporting Arius. The word selected in order to end the Arian controversy in fact complicated it.

It fell to Athanasius, Arius's junior by half a century, to defend the Nicene decree. At times he defended it almost by himself, *Athanasius contra mundum*, 'Athanasius against the world,' as the saying goes, although it should be said that if Arius was something more than the villain his critics have made him out to be, Athanasius was something less than the hero portrayed by his admirers, who tend to wink at the nastier side of his career. It remains that he was a thorn in the flesh of compromisers who wanted to hedge on doctrine for the sake of a little peace. He admitted that the *homoousios* was new. He agreed that it would have been better to stick to the words of Christian scripture. Unfortunately, he also pointed out, this route could no longer be taken. It had been blocked by the Arians, who were perfectly capable of construing in their own way all and any of the church's traditional statements about Christ. That had been their tactic at Nicea, and it left the assembled bishops no choice but to go outside scripture for an unequivocal expression. Thus according to Athanasius, who had been present as secretary to his own bishop, the council intended only to meet an emergency—not to set a precedent.

This part of his case for the Nicene decree amounts to making a virtue of necessity. One might still ask whether the *homoousios* makes matters as crystal clear as Athanasius claims it does. The answer depends on what you mean by 'substance.' If you mean stuff, something material and thus imaginable, you will find yourself back in Tertullian's difficulty. For if divine substance is a sort of supernal ectoplasm, you can only picture it as one cloud or as two. If one, you are saying that there is no real difference between the Father and his Son. They are a single quantity, which implies among other things that the Father was crucified. If on the other hand you imagine two clouds, you can say that they are consubstantial, of one substance, but you will also be saying that there are two Gods. Is there, then, a way to understand substance except as material, corporeal, and therefore imaginable? Athanasius manages to do it.

He starts not with stuff but with sunlight, which for years had been a very common metaphor for the relation of the Father and the Son. Everyone, Athanasius argues, would say that the sun and its radiance or brightness are two things rather than one, yet nobody would say that there are two lights, two substances. The radiance does not come afterwards; it is neither an addition to the sun nor another, different light; nor does it 'become' light, by participating in the light that is the sun. Rather, the sun generates brightness, gives birth to it, so that the brightness is in the fullest sense the sun's offspring—not separate from it, as children are separate from their parents, but one with it in being a single light. In the same way, the Father and the Son are two, yet there is only one deity. The Son is not an addition to the Father; his is neither a different divinity from the Father's nor, as Origen had taught, a divinity by participation. Father and Son are even more inseparable than sun and radiance; "why then should the Son not be called consubstantial with the Father?"

But that is only the beginning of Athanasius's argument. Even the image of sunlight is still an image. It can be useful in forming a preliminary notion of what *homoousios* might mean. But no image applies to God in the same way it applies to creatures. God is not imaginable—on that score, Origen was quite right. Accordingly, Athanasius continues, "just as we have no human thoughts when we say 'offspring,' and just as we entertain no material ideas about God though we know he is a Father . . . so in like manner, when we hear of 'consubstantial' we ought to pass beyond our senses."

Is anything left of the sunlight image, once we have thus transcended its imaginable content? Only this: as there is one light, belonging equally to the sun and its brightness, so there is one divinity (whatever that means—a crucial question) that is as much the Son's as the Father's. "And in a word, all that you find said of the Father you will equally find said of the Son; all, that is, except his being Father." To back up this final step of his argument, Athanasius adds a string of thirty quotations from scripture, grouping them in pairs to show that attributes of God are applied to Christ. Both are referred to as Lord, almighty, everlasting. To both are ascribed the forgiveness of sins and the raising of the dead. And so on.

Notice what Athanasius has done. His aim is to explain the vexatious word *homoousios*, 'consubstantial.' The familiar image he starts with *suggests* what he wants to say, but it needs to be qualified. Since God is invisible, the visual appeal of the image has to be distilled out. What is left is not an image at all. Consubstantiality is not a sensible quality, like greenness or bitterness. But neither is *homoousios* a flight of philosophical speculation about what God is in himself. As Athanasius interprets it, the Nicene doctrine means no more and no less than that whatever is *said* of the Father is likewise said of the Son, apart from the name 'Father.'

3

Here I must pause to introduce the third point of reference for this chapter. It is a two-line dialogue, invented but quite plausible, between a parent and a twelve-year-old.

PARENT (*somewhat put out*):   That was a very naughty
                                thing to do. Say you're
                                sorry.

CHILD (*impishly*):   You're sorry.

The twelve-year-old knows quite well that what 'Say you're sorry' calls for, in this context, is an apology. By responding as though 'Say you're sorry' meant 'Utter this sentence: *You're sorry*,' the exasperating child is showing off an ability that most children acquire at about the same age—the ability to talk about talk. Having known for years how to operate on words so as to assemble sentences, they find at the age of twelve or so that it is possible to operate on the sentences themselves. They can, for example, distinguish the form of the following sentence from its content.

It's a good thing I don't like broccoli,
because if I did like it I would always be eating it,
and I hate eating things that taste bad.

A younger child's response to this will be to say that it means 'broccoli tastes bad' or 'everybody ought to like broccoli,' whereas an adolescent will respond to the form of the sentence by pointing out the contradiction between 'if I did like it' and 'broccoli tastes bad.' There is nothing grammatically wrong with the sentence. It is assembled properly. Yet it doesn't 'make sense.' If I did like broccoli, then broccoli would *not* taste bad. The sentence as it stands is illogical.

Logic, in the most basic sense, is a technique that regulates meaning by operating on the propositions in which meaning is expressed. *Formal* logic is a set of rules that expand enormously on the twelve-year-old's ability to grasp the relation between one proposition and another, as for example between 'I like broccoli' and 'Broccoli tastes bad.' *If* either of these is true, the other is not. *Whether* either of them is true is not the point. Logic has to do with form, not content, and the formal validity of an argument does not depend on the truth of its component statements. Lewis Carroll, after making this important distinction, illustrates it as follows:

'I have sent for you, my dear Ducks,' said the worthy Mrs. Bond, 'to enquire with what sauce you would like to be eaten?' 'But we don't want to be *killed*!' cried the Ducks. '*You are wandering from the point*' was Mrs. Bond's perfectly logical reply.

If there is duck for dinner, then there will be sauce of one kind or another. Only the relation of the first proposition to the second is, logically speaking, relevant.

A further point can be made with another of Carroll's examples. Consider these three statements:

(1) Babies are illogical;

(2) Nobody is despised who can manage a crocodile;

(3) Illogical persons are despised.

If you infer from these that babies cannot manage crocodiles you are, logically, correct. You arrived at your inference by thinking in a certain way. Formal logic simply sets out in generally applicable terms the shape of the thinking you used on this particular example. The 'rules' of logic are like the rules of chess. Some moves are valid, others not. The difference is that someone invented the movement of chess-pieces, whereas the movements that formal logic codifies are operations of the human mind.

Presumably, people have been operating on propositions for nearly as long as they have used language to frame the propositions they have operated on. But they have not always been aware that this is what they were doing. Logic, in the formal sense, was a discovery—and a momentous one. It took place in Greece, some twenty-three hundred years ago. Here, as Northrop Frye describes it,

> the intellectual operations of the mind become distinguishable
> from the emotional operations; hence abstraction becomes
> possible, and the sense that there are valid and invalid ways of
> thinking, a sense which is to a degree independent of our feelings,
> develops into the conception of logic.

What the Greeks discovered was that they could more readily say what they meant by saying it logically. To the pithy sayings, wise proverbs, and edifying tales that had guided human living in Greece as elsewhere, they added intelligent definitions, reasonable argument, precise distinctions. None of these replaced the ordinary language of common sense; they added a set of techniques for reflecting on it. And, to return to the beginning of this section, all of these techniques are variations on a theme, the proposition *about* propositions. The twelve-year-old in my dialogue was not using formal logic, but he was on the right track. By themselves, the three words *say you're sorry* can be construed as a sentence *about* a sentence. 'Say: *You're sorry*' is a sentence about the sentence 'You're sorry.'

The child may never know what a useful tool the proposition about propositions can be, since formal logic is not often included in today's school curriculums, but he will be using such propositions for the rest of his life. 'We hold these truths to be self-evident' is a proposition about all the propositions that follow it in the Declaration of Independence. 'Jones said exactly what Smith did' is a proposition about whatever propositions were uttered by Smith and Jones. 'Anything you say may be held against you in a court of law' is a proposition about propositions that have yet to be made. All of these examples are 'second-level propositions.' The fact that none of them is particularly abstruse only goes to show that logic—not in the sense of syllogism and deduction, but in the more basic sense of talk about talk—is still very much alive. If nothing else had survived from the Greek 'discovery of mind,' the logical technique of the second-level proposition has.

From what I have said so far it might be thought that I want to have my cake and eat it too. In chapter four I pointed out the logical layout of theology as practiced in the 'house of authority,' and hinted (though I have not finished following up the hint) that this layout is a major shortcoming. Just now, on the other hand, I have been praising logic as an important and permanent achievement. But in fact it does work both ways. Logic *is* a good thing—only not everything. It does provide a way of expressing more clearly and consistently what we mean when we are thinking intelligently and reasonably. That having been said, it is also true that logic in itself is just the art of marking time. It lets us say the same thing in different words. They may be better words, less ambiguous and more intelligible, but they enhance only the form, not the content, of what we say. Logic is not everything, and three comments on why it is not will bring this section to a close.

In the first place, logic is merely a technique, an aid to clear thinking and not a substitute for it. Finally, as Newman said, "It is the mind that reasons, and that controls its own reasonings, not any technical apparatus of words and propositions."

Second, and more important, logic by no means exhausts the mind's repertoire of activities. It cannot, by itself, generate new ideas, or produce invention or discovery or originality, or compel the ecstatic moment of finally getting the point. In sum, nothing that makes for *change* in the human world of meaning comes about by logic alone.

Third, and most important of all, the apparatus of formal logic has to have something to work on. It draws out the implications of more basic, 'logically prior' statements. These, in turn, may be implied by statements more basic still. Where does the sequence begin? That is the hoary question of first principles, the bedrock propositions from which all others logically follow. Since first principles, in this sense, are as it were outside the machine, logic cannot derive them. They have to be chosen, and choosing them is itself a matter not of intelligence but of wisdom. If you push this one step further back and ask how a wise person is to be distinguished from a fool, the only answer is one that was given earlier in a different connection: it takes one to know one. Wisdom is a quality of persons, not arguments; it is recognized by persons in other persons. To demand an extrinsic yardstick, syllogistic logic for example, is to trivialize the whole matter. The criteria of wisdom, without which reasoning cannot begin, are incarnate. There are no others.

What I have been saying, then, amounts to this. The Greek 'discovery of mind' marks the turning of a corner and the opening up of all sorts of new possibilities—but there are other corners to be turned. All the stock examples are still valid; if every human being is mortal and Socrates is human, then Socrates (unless he has already done so) will die. To know that Socrates is mortal, however, is a far cry from knowing who Socrates was, whether he was wise, or what the whole of Western civilization owes to his stubbornness in refusing to stop asking questions. Such knowledge depends, not on logic alone, but on reconstructing the human past.

4

My three points of reference have led in rather different directions. I have said something about how scholars do their work, about a controversial decision taken at Nicea in 325, and about the logical technique of second-level propositions. All of these converge on a problem that was mentioned, briefly, in chapter four. John Henry Newman was among the first to bring this problem into the open and attempt a solution, and the name he used for it, 'development of doctrine,' has stuck. It was not a wholly new problem. In one sense Newman asked the same question that prompted the medieval compendiums of Christian teaching: how can all the many and various doctrines comprised in Christian tradition be reconciled? The big difference is that the scholastic theologians regarded this as on the whole a philosophical question, whereas in the nineteenth century it was beginning to be seen as a historical one. Even that was not an altogether novel insight. The controversy that splintered the church in the sixteenth century began partly because attention had been called to differences between the official teaching of the time, and what had apparently been taught in the earliest days of Christianity. Still, it is one thing to recognize a difference, another to pin it down precisely, and yet another to account for it. No one in the sixteenth century supposed for a moment that the Christian message itself changes; the question was therefore where the message could be found. One side appealed to scripture as the only permanent source, the other to an ensemble of sources.

Since the rise of critical history, neither of these appeals has gone unchallenged. Each of them has had to face a difficulty that can be stated in a dozen words:

Every expression of meaning is relative to a context, and contexts change.

If this statement seems obvious, that is an indication of how far we have all become historically minded. Today it is possible to take for granted that people speak and write for their contemporaries, who may be quite different from ourselves. The world in which a Victorian novel, say, was written and read is not so different from ours as to preclude our entering it imaginatively, but it is different enough to seem quaint. We do not yet have to call in professional historians to elucidate what the novelist meant, but a few explanatory footnotes are usually helpful. And if we find ourselves thinking, 'How times have changed,' we are thinking in a way that in itself shows how far times *have* changed. For the very idea that times change is comparatively new. *Things* change; that has always been evident. Institutions, states, and communities are born and pass away. Yet all of this could be regarded, from what I have called the classicist point of view, as happening within the stable framework of a world in which there are fixed points of reference.

I have already suggested that a classicist view of human meaning and value is the terrain on which Christian theologians have built their systems for hundreds of years. Although modern science robbed this style of architecture of its prestige, it was still being used to build 'houses of authority' when modern historical scholarship began to erode the ground they were built on. Theologians could bar the doors, shut the windows, sit tight, and wait for the storm to pass. Some of them are still waiting. Or, they could take seriously what historians were discovering about the *pastness* of Christian sources. Taking this seriously would mean acknowledging that the Christian message, God's word though it may well be, was first announced in a particular context, a time and place and world of meaning quite different from the world of Athanasius, the world of Thomas Aquinas, the world of Luther, and very different from the world of today. To put it another way, what the Christian message means, what it is about, may indeed be eternal truth, God's plan for the salvation of the world. But a truth can be eternal only in an eternal context, of which there is only one—the mind of God. Where human minds are concerned, truth has to be expressed within some horizon, some construction of the human spirit. There have been contexts that have endured for a long time, classicism itself being a notable example. But none of them is eternal.

Thus the problem of reconciling the many expressions of Christian meaning takes on, as it were, a new dimension, the dimension of time. Because contexts change, a statement that was meaningful *then*, relevant and intelligible in its own setting, is not always or necessarily meaningful *now*. Times have changed. If Christian doctrines are to be understood at all, they will have to be understood in their proper surroundings, rather than as independent and permanently valid blossoms that can be snipped off here and there and gathered into a nosegay.

This was the challenge to the 'house of authority' that Newman faced. He saw that historians were no longer content simply to pass on 'that which hath received the approbation of so many.' They were adopting critical procedures. As Newman puts it, "the documents and the facts of Christianity have been exposed to a jealous scrutiny; works have been judged spurious which once were received without a question; facts have been discarded or modified which were once first principles in argument; new facts and new principles have been brought to light." As a result, the teachings of Christianity "present a less compact and orderly front to the attacks of its enemies now than formerly, and allow of the introduction of new inquiries and theories concerning its source and its rise." In a word, the traditional coherence of theology was dissolving, because authoritative statements of doctrine were being treated not as statements but as evidence.

Evidence for what? Newman's sense of history was strong enough for him to recognize that this was the crucial question. And he saw that it was not to be answered by repeating the dictum of Vincent of Lérins. The unity of Christian teaching could not, in any straightforward way, be identified with 'what has been believed everywhere, always, and by all.' The evidence was evidence for variety and change. But, Newman replied, the changes themselves have a pattern, a wholeness, a unity that he was fond of comparing to the growth of a living organism. Christian doctrine had *developed*.

This is not the place to explore the arguments Newman offers in defense of his thesis. The gist of them all is that change does not have to be equated with error, Vincent notwithstanding. If anything, Newman was inclined to think that the development of Christian doctrine, considered on the whole, has been improvement. But he was not very consistent on the point, and it is in any case open to two criticisms. One was made almost before the ink was dry on the pages of his *Essay on the Development of Christian Doctrine*. It is all very well to say, as Newman does, that "to live is to change, and to be perfect is to have changed often." But to be decadent is also to have changed often. Deformation, corruption, disintegration, and the like—these are just as much developments, patterns of change, that is, as are ripening and maturation and progress. By what criteria, then, shall positive developments be distinguished from negative ones?

Newman does provide tests of authentic development, seven of them. The fact that they do not work as well as he thought they do suggests the second and more fundamental criticism that can be levelled at his *Essay*. Owing to a personal crisis of his own, a question of confessional allegiance, Newman was especially concerned to show that there had been a development, not developments, in Christian doctrine. He attempted to take the whole range of Christian tradition into account—itself a traditional goal—by bringing it all under one theory of development; more accurately, under a set of overlapping theories. Following his lead, many later theologians have similarly tried to fit all the evidence into one kind of pattern.

Here the difficulty is more subtle. It is not that a historical investigation, which is what Newman wanted his *Essay* to be, should proceed without any prior notion of what there is to be investigated. That is the 'principle of the empty head,' which I have already said is a myth. The point is rather that theories have to be tested against the available evidence, and changed, if need be, as the investigation goes on. Whether there has been one kind of development or several cannot simply be decided in advance; it depends on the results of scholarly labor on an enormous amount of evidence. Newman was not equipped for this job; no one person is. Not surprisingly, he tends to fit the facts to his theory rather than the other way round.

A better way to approach the problem of development would be to ask how it is possible that Christian doctrine has changed. If the Christian message is indeed the word of God, a communication of specific meaning and not just a symbolic reflection on the general religiousness of the human race; if it is a 'revelation,' to use a much debated theological term, how can human minds develop it? How can they improve, so to speak, on God? The answer, I would say, is that they do not. They improve on themselves. The evidence for developments in Christian doctrine is evidence for developments in the thinking, understanding, and judging of the Christian community. As many as these changes have been, so many are the possible kinds of doctrinal development. Thus the particular case of development that I outlined— no more than that—in the second section of this chapter illustrates the turning of a particular corner. By adopting the Nicene decree, the church changed itself and at the same time introduced its teaching about Christ into a new context. In the next section I will try to explain how this occurred. It should be noted, however, that what was going on was only one kind of development, important but not exclusive of other kinds.

5

In one respect at least, Newman's handling of the problem of doctrinal development has been given the seal of approval by more recent scholars, even when they quarrel with him heartily on every other point. He concentrated on the patristic period, the time of the 'fathers of the church.' For, as one eminent historian has put it, these first six centuries are Christian doctrine's center of gravity. And the center of that center was the council of Nicea. It is still customary to divide the patristic writers, as in the most extensive English collection of their works, into ante-Nicene and post-Nicene fathers.

In part, the preeminence of the synod that met in 325 is a matter of how it came to be regarded by the Christian community that it helped to define. Later councils referred to it as 'the holy and great synod' and deferred to its doctrine; for example, the Chalcedonian definition that was quoted in chapter three endorses the 'creed of the fathers,' referring to the one drawn up at Nicea. In retrospect, Nicea was reckoned as the first 'general' council of the church, and its teaching the first 'dogma'—the first doctrine publicly and officially defined as such.

That has been the traditional view. Without necessarily contradicting it, historians will adopt a different one. They will want to understand what the Nicene watchword 'consubstantial' was evidence *for*. What was and had been happening? What changed? What was going on in the interval between what Pliny called hymns to Christ as a god, and the solemn declaration that the Lord Jesus Christ is of one Being with the Father?

The decision taken at Nicea is evidence for the answering of a question: that is the main point of my abbreviated account of what led up to the council. It was not the general question of Christ's relation to God the Father but the more specific one that Arius raised, the question whether Christ is a creature. It was in some sense inevitable that such a question should come up, since on one hand the title 'Son of God' had been given to Jesus from the first, while on the other the church maintained Judaism's strict doctrine of God's oneness. But there was an even more important reason. "That Jesus was Lord and therefore to be worshipped is the 'given,' more fundamental than any doctrine, from which Christology starts, but in the long run it required a doctrine to explain and support it." The Arian controversy, in other words, was not a game of theological Scrabble. When Athanasius championed the Nicene doctrine he was not merely contending for a word or a formula. He saw that the meaning of Arius's doctrine was at odds with the meaning latent in the church's worship. "We do not worship a creature," he writes. "Far be the thought. Such an error belongs to pagans and Arians."

This leads to a further point. Christ was Lord, and therefore to be worshipped, because of what he had done and was doing. For the Arians, he had only done what anyone, in principle, can do. The central point of their system, as a recent study puts it, was "that Christ gains and holds his sonship in the same way as other creatures," so that "what is predicated of the redeemer can and must be predicated of the redeemed." Athanasius, on the contrary, maintained that Christ had done and was doing what only God can do, so that what is predicated of *God* can and must be predicated of the redeemer. That is his 'rule' for interpreting the *homoousios*. As Athanasius reports the bishops' deliberations at Nicea, they went to scripture, collected a series of assertions about Christ, "and lastly they wrote, more plainly and concisely, that the Son is consubstantial with the Father, for that is what all these passages mean." The word is not important for its own sake. Salvation is. Arius (to put it in terms used in an earlier chapter) conceived salvation as a superior sort of formation. For Athanasius it was transformation, Christ's drawing of men and women into community with the very life of God. "For he became human so that we might become divine."

Three things remain to be said about the Nicene doctrine. The first is that, as the *homoousios* answered a question bound up with Christian worship, so too it returned to that context. As interpreted by Athanasius's little rule, it made its way into the church's eucharistic celebration as a preface, the first English version of which is the epigraph of this chapter. For nearly fourteen hundred years, until a different idiom was adopted late in the twentieth century, Christians professed in their corporate prayer that what they believe of the glory of the Father they believe also of the Son, without any difference or inequality.

The second thing to note is that while Nicea is important for having defined a particular doctrine, the way it was defined is even more important. This is where the present chapter's third point of reference comes in. By stating that the Son is consubstantial with the Father, the council was using one word as a kind of metaphorical shorthand for a statement about statements. *Homoousios* stands for a second-level proposition: all the predicates of God, except the name 'Father,' are also predicates of the Son. As I have tried to suggest, there is nothing very arcane about this. It amounts to saying in different words what Christianity was saying already. The rule of Athanasius is a logical rule, and as such it is entirely open ended. Like every other logical technique it concerns the form rather than the content of propositions. It says nothing about *which* attributes are to be assigned to the Father, and so also to the Son; "it leaves the believer free to conceive the Father in scriptural, patristic, medieval, or modern terms."

If that is really all that the *homoousios* means, what makes it so important? The answer is that at Nicea the church's teaching took the first step of entering a new context. Just as the discovery of logical techniques in general was a major achievement of the human mind, so the introduction of one such technique into Christian doctrine marks a turning point. It is not that the moving, imaginative language of scripture and the earlier fathers was jettisoned, any more than a twelve-year-old ceases to talk upon learning to talk *about* talk. Rather, the Christian message in all its richness began to be reflected on as well as proclaimed. The church went on teaching Christ, but in addition it examined, organized, and unified its teaching. Nicea was the first step in this direction. There would be many more.

6

Nothing stays put. This free translation of a saying by the ancient philosopher Heraclitus sums up the challenge presented to classicist theology by modern history. It is difficult to build a house if the bricks keep changing their places, and by now the whole Christian tradition—scripture, fathers, scholastics, reformers—has been taken to pieces for critical, scholarly scrutiny. One way of taking such historical scholarship seriously is to make it a kind of auxiliary to theology proper. Scholars, on this view, would continue their research, exegetes would endeavor to interpret what a given doctrine meant in its original context, and the result would be handed over to the historians. The question is what the theologians are to do with these results once they have them. The next step quite often rests on "the assumption that someone, somewhere, at some time in the past, really knew the truth, [and] that what we have to do is to find out what he thought and get back to it." It may be Luther who said the last word on what the Christian message is all about, or the author of the Gospel of John, or Thomas Aquinas—*someone* said it, and once historical scholarship has established just what that someone said and just what it meant, the rest is smooth sailing.

Or is it? The method I have just outlined, although it does take history seriously, still has a familiar ring. It is really the classicist appeal to authoritative sources, only now it has become an indirect appeal, filtered through scholarly channels. Providing the materials has been sub-contracted to others, but what will be built with them is still a 'house of authority.' The difficulty is that the study of history, since the advent of critical procedures, has become an ongoing process. Scholars arrive at tentative conclusions, only to have other scholars amplify, correct, or refute

them. Even the most definitive solution to a historical problem
raises a whole flock of new questions, and the process goes on.
Thus, even if someone, somewhere, at some time in the past,
really did know the truth, the last word has not been said on what
he knew.

That means—and it is the point of this whole chapter—that the
last word has not been said on any Christian doctrine. Doctrines
are not like buckets passed from hand to hand in a fire brigade.
They pass from mind to mind. The meaning of any doctrine, like
the scholarly procedures that disclose it, is a process, a history of
questions raised and answers given. I have painted the outline of
one part of one such process—the question about Christ's relation
to God the Father, Tertullian's answer, Origen's partial correction
of that kind of answer, Arius's putting of the question in a way
that had to be answered yes or no, Nicea's answer, and Athanasius's interpretation of it.

The doctrine that the Son is consubstantial with the Father
means all of that, but that is not all it means. No sooner had the
Nicene decree been accepted than a new series of questions arose,
the first one being whether the Holy Spirit too is consubstantial
with the Father. Each new question raised and each new answer
given changed the context in which Nicea's doctrine was understood. The process has marked time, but it has never stood still.
The scholastics raised new philosophical questions. Luther raised
the question of sources. Newman raised the question of development. What the *homoousios*, or any other doctrine, means is not
what it meant at any one point along the way. What it means is
what it has been meaning.

All of this may sound somewhat mystifying, but it is nothing
more than an application of what I proposed in chapter three:
Christian community and Christian doctrine are and always have
been reciprocal. As the community has grown and changed,
decayed and flourished, so has its teaching. Doctrines are not
like baggage but like blood; not objects extrinsic to the church
but intrinsic to its ongoing life. Does that imply that Christian

doctrines mean whatever the church decides they mean? It does, in a sense. But that it does is also the venerable doctrine according to which the *sensus fidelium*, the common meaning of the faithful, is the standard of Christian belief.

And does that, in turn, imply that the church, for all my talk about the Christian message, has all along been engaged in a conversation with itself? The answer depends on a further question. Does God too take history seriously, seriously enough to have entered into the conversation? To that question the next two chapters will turn.

❧ SIX ❧
Doctrines and Scripture

The work of revelation, like the whole work of Christ, is the work of the mystical Christ, who embraces both Head and members.

AUSTIN FARRER

AMONG THE TREASURES of a library in Dublin are the four volumes of what is probably the most celebrated book in the world. It was already famous in the twelfth century, when these admiring lines were written: "Examine it carefully and you will penetrate to the very shrine of art. You will make out intricacies so delicate and subtle, so exact and compact, so full of knots and links, with colors so fresh and vivid, that you might think all of this was the work of an angel."

The color has faded a bit on the pages of the Book of Kells, but each of them is embellished—and some of them are completely filled—with designs that combine geometrical precision and whimsical exuberance in a way that still gives the impression of more than human skill. And that raises a question: why? Why was such disciplined fancy, such painstaking inventiveness, lavished on a book? The result is magnificent—magnificently superfluous, from a utilitarian point of view. Simple black and white would have done for reading, which is ordinarily what books are for.

But then, the Book of Kells is no ordinary book. It was meant for reading, certainly; almost certainly for reading aloud. But that was not its only purpose. It was also an object of reverence. Between readings, it was displayed, open, so that anyone could tell from the splendor of its pages that it was different from other books. The artists who labored for years on the Book of Kells were no doubt fond of ornamentation. But people decorate what they cherish, and these scribes and painters cherished words. They made an extraordinary book, 'the very shrine of art,' to honor an extraordinary text. What they copied out in such elegant letters and enhanced with 'intricacies so delicate and subtle' was not just any writing. It was scripture, sacred writing.

The Book of Kells is a gospel-book. Its text is the Christian story, in the four versions known as the Gospels of Matthew, Mark, Luke, and John. Nothing was more important for the community that made and used this book than to read, mark, learn, and inwardly digest its words, and they did everything that ingenuity and craft could do in order to make the writing itself a visible expression of importance. This is especially evident in the full-page paintings at the beginning of each of the four gospels. In the first of them, most of the space is filled with an elaborate border composed of intricate knots and spirals and an endless chain of tiny reptiles, each meticulously coiled in its own tail. Even in reproduction the complexity of this frame is astonishing. Yet it serves to lead the eye again and again towards what it frames. At the center of the page sits a man, solemnly staring, a book in one of his hands. He is Matthew, the evangelist. The book he holds is his gospel, the first two words of which appear on the equally ornate page opposite his portrait.

It is less a portrait, though, than an icon. Neither the pose nor the features of the man it pictures suggests a 'realistic' likeness; they contribute instead to a mysterious image that evokes the awe and respect due to a saint who was also privileged to put the Christian message into human words. This striking page thus honors Matthew because of what he wrote; it honors what he wrote because of what it meant; and so the page itself and the book it was bound in shared in the reverence appropriate to the word of God.

A few paragraphs back, I asked what prompted a work of art like the Book of Kells, and my answer has been an exercise of historical imagination, a brief attempt to recapture something of the convictions and feelings that motivated unknown craftsmen some eleven centuries ago. What they made was a focus of regard—regard for the Christian gospel, for the inspired evangelists, for their message, for the text, and for the very letters that conveyed a divine communication. The Book of Kells was both the cause and the effect of the many-faceted esteem in which Christians have traditionally held their scriptures. And, like other traditions, the holiness of the Holy Bible has diminished in modern times; if not for individual Christians and their communities, certainly for the larger society they live in. For religious people the book itself is still an object of reverence, as it can be on certain secular occasions like the swearing-in of civil magistrates. But the same text also appears on the philosophy-and-religion shelves of book shops, bound in paper covers and treated as any other book would be.

Nor, more importantly, do the contents of the Bible occupy the unique place they once held. If Christendom is defined as a social, institutional, and political body of which Christian meaning and value are the soul, then Christendom is not what it was—not least because the Bible is not what it was. Whatever may be true of individuals and groups, Western culture as a whole does not seem to take its bearings from Christian scripture. I am not suggesting that people were more genuinely religious in times past; that is at best doubtful. What is not is that biblical images, biblical stories, and the overall pattern of the biblical narrative were, for much of Western history, woven into the fabric of everyone's life. When a seal was needed for the newly independent United States, one of the proposed designs showed the children of Israel crossing the Red Sea—a symbol of liberation from tyranny that no one would have to puzzle over. A century later, the same biblical story was being recalled in a different way:

Go down, Moses,
Way down in Egypt land.
Tell old Pharoah,
Let my people go!

As Northrop Frye observes, citing this example, "The Israelites were not black, and nineteenth-century American blacks had no quarrel with ancient Egypt. The point is that when any group of people feels as strongly about anything as slaves feel about slavery, history as such is dust and ashes." Only a 'saving tale,' a story with a transcendent dimension, can provide support and hope. The Book of Exodus is such a story. And everyone knew it.

But Frye also points out how unfamiliar the Bible has become. "Why," he asks, "does this huge, sprawling, tactless book sit there inscrutably in the middle of our cultural heritage . . . frustrating all our efforts to walk around it?" What is significant is that such a question has to be asked, and that it is being asked by a literary critic. The 'language' of the Bible (using that word in its broadest sense) pervades Western art and literature like a 'great code,' yet fewer and fewer people know the key. The Bible itself, to quote a theologian, "has become a great but archaic monument in our midst. It is a reminder of where we once were—but no longer are." This statement, which Gordon Kaufman makes in an article entitled "What Shall We Do With the Bible?", strikes the same metaphorical note as Frye's question: the Bible as a strange, massive presence, not understood yet not to be ignored. I suspect that Kaufman is overstating the situation. There are plenty of people for whom the Bible is not an enigma but a treasure, and who nourish their lives on its meaning. But they would perhaps be among the first to agree that they have this treasure in earthen vessels that interest many only as archaeological specimens and interest many others not at all.

Something has happened, something that Kaufman is pointing to in the phrase 'where we were—but no longer are.' If his 'we' is taken as referring to Western society across the board, he is right.

'Where we were' can be seen in medieval paintings of the kind that are reproduced on Christmas cards. They often show what musical instruments were like in the middle ages, because the angels have been provided with medieval viols and the shepherds with medieval bagpipes. Perhaps the painters were aware of the anachronism, but if so it did not matter. The episode they were depicting was part of a story that belonged to all time, a story whose characters were in some real way their contemporaries. Nor did this sense of timelessness end with the middle ages. When Rembrandt painted the nativity, he also painted a seventeenth-century Dutch family. W.H. Auden achieves the same kind of synthesis in his long Christmas poem, "For the Time Being." The speakers use a modern idiom, yet they are still the biblical figures and the story they take part in is still the biblical story; it all happened, long ago, and it is all happening, now.

Auden's poem, however, is something of a *tour de force.* To read it is to still, for the time being, what has been called modernity's sixth sense—the sense of history. More than anything else, perhaps, awareness that times change is the reason why many people find the Bible a closed book. It belongs to another age, a different world, and even those for whom it is not an archaic monument but a source of strength cannot help feeling its 'pastness.' That would be true of any ancient literature, of course, but the Bible presents special problems. It has been subjected to more and longer scholarly scrutiny than any other book. The methods of critical history have been applied to every verse by generations of exegetes and interpreters, all of them asking in one way or another, 'What is this statement evidence for?' The answers have been publicized and popularized, debated and defended, and while none of them commands universal agreement, their combined result has been to set the Bible, whole and parts, even more firmly in the past.

The effects of critical scholarship on classicist theology generally were discussed in the previous chapter: historians have dismantled the 'house of authority' and returned its materials, scripture included, to their proper surroundings. But biblical scholarship, New Testament studies in particular, raises questions that have a special bearing on all of Christian doctrine, in so far as they are questions about the story of Jesus.

2

New Testament scholarship is no game for amateurs. Even more than other fields of scholarly investigation, it is specialized and subdivided to the point that even the experts have a hard time finding their way around. Because they bring their expertise to bear on the message that constitutes Christian people, Christian tradition, and the Christian church *as* Christian, the work of these specialists has a relevance that extends beyond the academic community. In itself, however, New Testament scholarship is concerned with specific and often very technical questions. By way of example, take the text that stands first in the Book of Kells, and apply the question that I explored in the previous chapter: for what is the Gospel of Matthew evidence?

The first thing a historian would find important is that the text of the Gospel of Matthew exists in more than one version, and that unlike the text of the United States Constitution, say, there is no 'original' to serve as a standard of comparison. Even the earliest documents that contain the text of Matthew are handwritten copies of handwritten copies. Quite possibly, then, the differences between the various versions are evidence for scribal errors; possibly too, emendations have been made at points along the way. Every variation has to be considered separately, and the task of establishing the best reading, if not the 'original,' becomes a very complicated one in itself. For the sake of argument, however, let it be supposed that for the passages I will examine here, the work of textual criticism, as it is called, has already been done.

Returning to the original question, what is the text of Matthew, once it has been established, evidence for? Presumably it is evidence for somebody's having composed it in the first place. But this seemingly obvious point is far from trivial. The question of what 'composed' means, applied to the gospels, is a thorny one. That the Gospel of Matthew is similar to both the Gospel of Mark and the Gospel of Luke critics have long recognized. All three have the same general scope and outline, and for that reason are referred to as the 'synoptic' gospels. But often the similarity is more striking. The same episodes are related in the same or almost the same words, in the same order. There are enough of these verbal similarities to raise the question whether they are evidence for some kind of direct literary dependence, permissible plagiarism as it were. Parts of Matthew might have been taken more or less intact from Mark, or Luke, or both; or Matthew itself may have been the source of excerpts included in one or both of the others; or perhaps there was once another source, for which no documentary evidence now exists. Once the general idea of literary borrowing is admitted as a possible explanation, it can be made more specific in a large, though finite, number of ways. All of them are perfectly logical, although not all of them have been seriously proposed.

The problem of accounting for these verbal similarities is called the 'synoptic problem.' Unanimity has yet to emerge on all its aspects, but there is at least one thing about which a substantial majority of New Testament scholars agree. It is extremely probable that the Gospel of Mark is the oldest of the synoptics, and that Matthew is partly a reworking and partly an expansion of Mark. This hypothesis accounts for the relevant features of the textual evidence in a convincing way, but since the argument for it rests on the cumulative weight of many separate details, I cannot attempt to summarize it here. If this explanation is correct, what does it do to the man with the book portrayed so impressively in the Book of Kells? The inspired evangelist is demoted to the status of an editor, adapter, and general refurbisher of someone else's writing. He may only have put the finishing touches on the work of other revisers. 'He' may even have been 'they,' a kind of editorial committee. In any case, the composition of the gospel that bears his name seems, at least in part, to have been a process that New Testament scholars can reconstruct in purely human terms.

Such a conclusion cannot but affect a doctrine that was mentioned in chapter four as being 'foundational' for classicist theology—the doctrine of inspiration. In the words of one of the patristic writers, inspiration is like "a piper blowing on a flute." God does all the work; the person he inspires is just an instrument. But it seems that whoever put the Gospel of Matthew into its final shape was taking a more active part than that. What this implies for the way inspiration is understood will be considered later; for now, what matters is that seeing the text of the Gospel of Matthew as evidence for a certain kind of literary activity also has implications for how one construes it as evidence for the words and deeds of Jesus. Scholarly conclusions about how the text was written raise questions pertaining to what it was written about.

Only a specific example can show why this is so. According to the Gospel of Mark, Jesus, on the Sunday before he was crucified, entered Jerusalem riding on a colt which he had sent two of his disciples ahead to bring from the city (Mk 11:1-10). This episode as it appears in the Gospel of Matthew is almost identical, except for two additions, a detail and a comment. The detail is that Jesus tells the disciples to find an ass as well as a colt. The text, taken literally, goes on to say that he was seated on both of them as he entered Jerusalem (Mt 21:7). Is this curious detail of any importance? Is it evidence?

Such a question is on the same order as the one that Collingwood's detective asked about the rector's daughter's confession. That she made it because she was guilty was one, but not the only, possible answer. Similarly, the statements in Matthew about an ass *and* a colt could very well be there because Jesus did ride two animals. Perhaps he entered the city twice, once as reported in Mark and once as in Matthew. Or perhaps the account in Matthew is correct and the one in Mark is mistaken. But a further difference between the two suggests an explanation of quite a different sort. Here is Matthew's second addition: "This happened so as to fulfill the prophet's words, *Tell the daughter of Zion, 'See! Your king is coming to you, meek and mounted on an ass and on a colt, an ass's foal'* " (Mt 21:4-5). This is one of many such comments. Interrupting the narrative of Jesus' life and death with quotations to show how things happened 'so as to fulfill the prophet's words' is typical of what might be called the Matthean manner. 'Matthew' (whoever he was) would have his readers know that in Jesus what had been prophesied came to pass—in every detail.

Once the importance that 'Matthew' attached to this theme has been recognized, it becomes possible to ask whether he might have touched up the Gospel of Mark here and there, so as to bring the story more unmistakably into line with the prophecies he is so fond of quoting. To put it bluntly, did he supply the somewhat incongruous ass because an ass had been foretold? What is important about such a question is that it introduces a distinction between two things, what 'Matthew' meant by setting down certain words, and what Jesus actually did. In turn, this distinction rests on another, the distinction between a statement as statement, and the same statement as evidence. For critical historians, as I have already pointed out, statements *may* be evidence for what they are about, but they *are*, in the first instance, evidence about the people who made them. Thus the statement in Matthew *may* be evidence for details of Jesus' final entry into Jerusalem, but in the first instance it *is* evidence about 'Matthew,' or about the community in and for which he was writing, or (as is most likely) about both. Just as Collingwood's detective wanted to know what the rector's daughter meant by saying what she did, so New Testament scholars want to know what 'Matthew' was up to.

Among other things, he was rewriting the Gospel of Mark; that is pretty much agreed, and the passage under consideration is one of many that support it. But there is more to be said. Rewriting is a purposeful activity. It can be done for a variety of reasons. Which of them accounts for the alterations that 'Matthew' made? What did he mean by making them?

For a start, he meant what he believed. The text as it stands is first-hand evidence for conviction on the part of 'Matthew' and his community that the man who rode into Jerusalem was indeed Messiah, the anointed, the king whom the prophets looked and longed for, making a royal entry into his capital. This episode, like the rest of the story of Jesus, is told in the Gospel of Matthew so as to convey its religious significance to readers steeped in the same prophetic writings that are alluded to, if not quoted, on every page. By spelling it out from time to time, 'Matthew' emphasizes what Christians had believed from the first—that the story of Jesus continues and brings to its climax the story told in what is now called the Old Testament. That belief is not only stated but also embodied, given a narrative shape, throughout the Gospel of Matthew.

And what of the question about what actually occurred— was there only a colt, or was there an ass too? Nothing much hangs, one way or another, on whether the ass is a product of Matthean invention. But the same sort of question can be asked elsewhere, and it becomes more difficult to answer in those parts of the Gospel of Matthew which are not reworkings of Mark. Only in Matthew, for example, is there an account of the flight into Egypt, which includes the jealous king Herod's attempt to kill the child Jesus by ordering a general execution of boys two years old and younger. Did that happen?

The answer depends on several considerations. For one thing, the great Old Testament figure Moses, as every reader of Matthew would have known, similarly escaped a wholesale infanticide commanded by a jealous monarch. Is 'Matthew' deliberately setting up a symbolic parallel between Moses and Jesus? And if so, how much of the story is saying something about Jesus in a symbolic way, and how much of it represents what Herod actually did? As it happens, there is evidence apart from the New Testament for the events of Herod's reign. He was notoriously brutal. Yet among the many atrocities blamed on him there is no slaughter of babies. If such a thing did occur, it is not likely to have gone without comment. On the other hand, almost a third of this episode as it appears in Matthew consists of three Old Testament quotations, each introduced by a variation on the characteristic formula, 'This happened to fulfill the prophet's words.' Moreover, the theme of Jesus as a new and greater Moses recurs throughout the rest of the gospel.

All of this begins to suggest that 'Matthew,' whatever he was up to, was not writing straight factual history. But it would be a mistake to conclude that he must therefore have been writing pure fiction. Such a conclusion rests on the premise that narrative can only do one of two things: either it states what actually occurred, or it states what has not occurred at all. Put this way, the premise is manifestly false. Narrative is the most versatile form of expression there is. A distinction can and should be drawn between critical history and evaluative history, for example, but the distinction itself is quite recent. 'Matthew' did not draw it; none of the gospel-writers did. Probably they would not have known how to draw it had they wanted to, and there is no reason to suppose that they wanted anything of the sort. They had better things to do. They were writing from faith to faith, handing on a message, not handing out information. There is no historical fact in the gospels which is there *simply* because it is a historical fact. Everything is presented as what the earliest Christian communities discerned and believed it to have been.

Not that it is an easy matter to understand what exactly the primitive church did believe. The outline of the story by which the early Christians lived is straightforward enough. But the outline is filled in with such a profusion of imagery, metaphor, typology, symbolism, allusion, and numerology as to demand all the interpretive skill that scholars can muster. A whole world has to be reconstructed, a strange and subtle world to which the antithesis of fiction or fact applies about as well as it does to

a love-letter. This leads to a further, and in the present context
more important, general implication of considering the gospels
as first-hand evidence for early Christian belief: only indirectly
are they evidence for what Jesus did and said.

The whole quest for the historical Jesus comes down to one
basic question. Given what can be understood about the beliefs
of the earliest Christians, how is their belief to be accounted for?
Why did they believe what they did? The question admits of a
wide range of perfectly plausible answers, none of which ought
to be dismissed out of hand. At one end of the spectrum is the
view that the primitive church believed what it did because that
is what happened. What the gospels say about Jesus is accurate
word for word. At the other end is the view that the earliest
Christians were thoroughly deluded. Jesus never existed; the
whole story was dreamed up by his putative disciples. These
extreme positions, the one uncritical and fundamentalistic, the
other skeptical and rationalistic, are neither of them impossible.
As for the first, however, the well-known discrepancies between
and within the gospel narratives are against it, and as for the
second, how likely is it that the disciples were both shrewd
enough to fabricate a story that changed the world and also
simple enough to given someone else the credit? Between the
two, of course, there is a lot of room for a less simplistic position, although finding one is a complicated business.

What needs to be stressed, however, is that those who hold
some intermediate view are in the same precarious boat as those
who opt for one of the extremes. *Every* answer to the question
of who the Jesus of history was (or was not) is an inference from
the available data. But the only data available are data on early
Christian belief; no reconstruction of the historical Jesus can be
anything but a more or less convincing explanation of why those
data exist; and such historical inferences, as I pointed out in
chapter five, are seldom final. The past does not change, but our
understanding of it does. The explanations that critical historians
arrive at are constantly being revised, not because definitive

understanding is impossible in principle—it is not—but because what historians endeavor to understand is enormously complex. Thus Albert Schweitzer thought to bring the quest for the historical Jesus to an end by arguing that nothing at all can be said about him. Yet historians have not accepted Schweitzer's conclusion as definitive; the quest he laid to rest has taken a new lease on life, and is likely to outlive all of us.

In the nature of the case, then, the Jesus of history can be known only by inference, and tentative inference at that. But there is more to be said. Humphrey Palmer, in an excellent book on the logic of gospel criticism, points out that all we hear in a telephone conversation is a pattern of vibrations; strictly speaking, we can only infer, from the evidence available to our ears, that somewhere a friend is talking. Yet we all distinguish quite easily between the friend's voice and the noise that may accompany it. "The early Christians," Palmer continues, "may be responsible for a modicum of 'noise' on our only line to the Jesus of history. But through the crackling all later generations have made out their master's voice." His point is well taken, and cuts two ways. It is clear that the Christ portrayed in the gospels is the Christ believed in and proclaimed by the primitive church. Where—and whether—a line should be drawn between this 'Christ of faith' and the historical Jesus is not an impersonal question. What you think of Christ depends on what you think of the early Christians. The judgment that what they said is 'noise' is a judgment on them, an imputation of credulity or pious exaggeration or superstition.

In order to make such a judgment, however, you must presumably know what the early Christians were credulous of, what they exaggerated, what they were superstitious about. In other words, what you think of the Christians by and for whom the gospels were written depends on what you think of Christ. If he was not what they believed him to be, he was something else, something that you are capable of recognizing between the lines of the story they told about him. Jesus the teacher of an

enlightened ethical individualism, it may be; or Jesus the revolu-
tionary champion of oppressed peoples; Jesus the mystic, or Jesus
the magician, Jesus the madman or the Messiah. That is the point
of the famous quip about a great liberal theologian of the nineteenth century, who peered down a well of darkness in search
of the historical Jesus and saw, reflected through nineteen
hundred years, the face of a liberal theologian—his own.

Certainly that can happen. Historians are as prone as anyone
else to overlook what does not fit with their own views and
feelings, their own values and beliefs, their own horizons of
meaning. What they do not overlook, they can still misunderstand, and what they do not misunderstand they can still dismiss
as false or condemn as worthless. In short, historians do not shed
their own personal histories when they reconstruct what other
minds and hearts have constructed. All of this has been discussed
in the previous chapter; it follows from the fact that understanding the human past depends on understanding human beings.
But I have also emphasized that encountering the past is a two-
way affair, a merging of two horizons. As Collingwood writes of
the historian at work, "In re-thinking what somebody else
thought, he thinks it himself. In knowing that somebody else
thought it, he knows that he himself is able to think it." The
historian's own horizon changes. It expands to include new
ideas, new hopes and fears, new possibilities. The strangeness of
a distant world of meaning can itself challenge the historian's
world, alter it, even dismantle it. Instead of seeing their own
personalities reflected from the bottom of a well of time, scholars
who plunge themselves in the past may find that they emerge
with a completely new outlook on the present. They may, to
return to Palmer's metaphor, hear their master's voice through
the crackling.

Such can be the result of encountering the world of the
earliest Christians. Doubtless it is a strange world. The whole
New Testament is evidence for thoughts that are not our usual
thoughts and ways that are not our customary ways. Because

its 'pastness' is undeniable, there are some who would contend that the New Testament cannot be taken seriously, and others who would argue that taking it seriously is somehow morally wrong, as though the first and great commandment were, 'Be modern—whatever it costs.' But neither the moral nor the intellectual horizon of modern times is any more fixed and immutable than others have been. On the contrary, our world of meaning is a kaleidoscope of competing ideas and values, a babel of voices shrilly demanding our attention. The Christian message may be difficult to hear amid this clamor of claims and counterclaims, all the more difficult in that historical scholarship has widened the 'gap between the centuries.' Yet that gap is not unbridgeable. The gospels, for all their pastness, do transform the present lives of men and women. And when they do, it is primarily because they remain today what they were written to be—a story.

3

Before going any further, I need to gather the threads of my discussion so far. I began this chapter with the Book of Kells, a visible expression of the idea that the Christian gospel is a truth valid for all time. Times have changed, though, and a general awareness that times do change is one of the reasons why it is difficult for many people to feel themselves at home in the world of the Bible. Their historical sense gets in the way. Moreover, the development and specialization of this 'sixth sense' by modern scholarship raises a cloud of questions about the historical accuracy of the Bible in general and the gospels in particular, some of which cast a skeptical shadow on the way scripture has long been used by the Christian community as a basis of its doctrine. In the second section of this chapter I outlined the basic issue: the gospels are first-hand evidence for early Christian belief and second-hand evidence for the process by which they were composed; only indirectly do they provide evidence for the Jesus of history. No historical event found its way into the gospels solely in virtue of being a historical event, because the gospels are 'salvation history.' Each is a personal address in narrative form, written from faith to faith. And since the personal dimension counts even more than in some investigations of the past, how the Christian message is understood as evidence depends on how it is responded to as an address.

No one has made this point better than Schweitzer did in the famous lines at the end of his *Quest of the Historical Jesus.* Jesus comes to us, he writes, "as of old, by the lake-side, he came to those who did not know him. He speaks to us the same word: *Follow me!* . . . And to those who obey him, be they wise or simple, he will disclose himself in the toils, the conflicts, the sufferings they will pass through." The message of the gospels is a call for decision, intensely personal and thoroughly radical. 'Resist not evil.' 'It is more blessed to give than to receive.' 'Forgive the person who offends you, not once or even seven times a day, but seventy times seven.' 'If your coat is stolen, give the thief your shirt too.' 'Love your enemies, do good to those who hate you.' 'Turn the other cheek.' 'Sell all you have, leave parents and family, shoulder your cross day by day—and follow me.'

One of the earliest critics of Christianity, the philosopher Celsus, found it especially offensive that 'Follow me' is not an intellectual precept. It might be addressed to anyone, wise or simple, as indeed it is. Those who respond to it have been addressed by a story. The whole gospel, to use Eric Voegelin's term, is a 'saving tale,' a narrative about what it calls 'blessedness' and the 'kingdom of God'; about an 'abundant life' that is not a possession but a gift to be embraced—by dying. To respond to this message, then, is to act. How? That is a further question. According to the sequel of the Gospel of Luke, the Acts of the Apostles, just such a question was asked by some of those who heard the story about Jesus as it was being preached for the first time by one of those who followed him. Hearing this recital, "they were cut to the heart. 'What shall we do?' they said" (Ac 2:37). Their question was itself an engaged response, not a cool speculative inquiry. The story had spoken to their condition; they were asking about a message that had become a message *for them.*

There were other questions to be asked, questions of a different kind, questions that are asked still by those whom the story of Jesus has cut to the heart. 'Follow me' invites action, and it invites personal commitment as well. It calls for a decision to live in a certain way, and also a decision *for* a certain person— the person whom the gospels portray as the source of their unsettling view of what constitutes the best way to live.

Who, then, is Jesus?

That question runs through the gospels. "Who is this, that even the wind and sea obey him?" (Mk 4:41). "Who is the man who said to you, 'Take up your bed and walk'?" (Jn 5:12). "How can you say that the Son of man must be lifted up? Who is this Son of man?" (Jn 12:34). Jesus asks it himself. After listening to the general run of opinion about himself, he says to those who have decided to follow him, "But who do *you* say that I am?" One of them, Peter, gives a response that is as well known as anything in the New Testament: "You are the Christ, the Son of the living God!" (Mt 16:15-16). Three observations on Peter's acclamation are in order.

The first concerns what Jesus is reported as saying to him immediately afterwards. It was not flesh and blood—not popular opinion, and not Peter's own reasoning—that had disclosed Jesus' identity. It was the God whom Jesus called Father. This speech expands the earlier version of Peter's confession that appears in the Gospel of Mark, and so all the usual difficulties can be raised about whether the historical Jesus uttered it. They do nothing, however, to change the status of the speech as first-hand evidence for what 'Matthew' and his community believed, namely that people do not arrive at the assertion 'Jesus is the Christ, the Son of the living God' under their own steam. Those who say it, and mean what they say, are saying it because they, like Peter, have already decided to follow Jesus and are being drawn to acclaim him by his Father.

More on this presently. The second observation is that Peter's acclamation uses two of many titles, some fifty-five according to one count, applied to Jesus in the New Testament. Some of these titles, embodied in short exclamations such as 'Jesus is Lord,' were probably the earliest statements of Christian belief. Around this nucleus summaries of the Christian message were formulated, and eventually the gospels themselves were written to give these formulas a narrative context in which they could be properly understood. This scholarly reconstruction of the earliest phases of development in Christian doctrine implies that the old question of how the Proclaimer became the Proclaimed has got things backwards. Christ was first proclaimed; narratives about the Proclaimer came later.

This leads to my third observation. A context for understanding the proclamation was added because it is one thing to affirm that Jesus is the Christ, the Son of the living God, and quite another to understand what such an affirmation means. The episode just after Peter's affirmation, taken as evidence, suggests that misunderstandings did occur. Jesus begins to teach that he would have to suffer, and be killed, and rise. Peter finds this unacceptable. Jesus tells him that *he* is unacceptable: "Get behind me, you Adversary! You are a hindrance to me, for you"—Peter, whom Jesus had just blessed for his God-given acclamation—"you are not on the side of God but of men" (Mt 16:23). Much has been made of the secret that Jesus is reported to have made of his being the Messiah, the Christ. In this passage, however, it is not the title itself but what the title means that calls for discretion and discernment. A Messiah without suffering, 'Matthew' insists, is not what the Christian message is about.

The reader will have noticed that although I began this section by stressing the impact of the gospels as a personal message, I have come round to examining specific texts in the scholarly way, that is, as evidence for early Christian belief. The sequence is important. In the gospel narrative, Jesus' message is a personal invitation—as it still is. In the gospel narrative, the lives of those who accept the invitation are changed—as they still are. In the gospel narrative, living out one's commitment to Jesus raises the further question, 'Who *is* he?'—as it still does. All of which implies what I said at the end of the previous section: this question is not independent of the questioner. It makes a difference whether you ask 'Who is Jesus?' as someone whose being the gospel has touched; whether it is in any sense a message *for you*; whether you would have its story be yours; in sum, whether or not your question is about the Jesus whom the New Testament presents as the source of what it has to say about salvation. As it takes a reasonable person to discern what a reasonable judgment is, a good person to discern what good conduct is, a person in love to discern what the signs of lovableness are, so too it takes a religious person to discern what pertains to salvation, transformation, 'new life.'

But what I have just proposed needs to be clarified. It may look as though I am throwing objective impartiality to the winds. So I am, if impartiality means indifference and being objective is the same as denying who you are. On the other hand, I am not by any means suggesting that the thing to do is first make up your mind about what pertains to salvation and then go and see whether it is in the New Testament. Probably it is; most things are, if you look hard enough. But why even bother with the New Testament if your mind is made up already? That approach is a sure recipe for obscurantism, and the argument of the previous paragraph is rather different. It comes down to this. All that scholarship can do should be done to shed light on what the early church believed, but no amount of scholarly acumen can, by itself, effect the transition from 'The early church believed such-and such' to 'I believe it,' or from 'According to so-and-so in the first century, this is what pertains to salvation' to 'This *is* what pertains to salvation.'

On any showing, the early Christians had something over-
poweringly important to say, something they were convinced
was true, valuable as well as true, and holy as well as valuable.
What it was can be discerned in so far as it has begun to overpower
you. If it has not, you will be content with indirect discourse—
'this is what they *said* was true, or good, or holy.' If it has, you
will have begun to make their affirmations your own.

4

What has any of this to do with doctrines?

The question is a broad one, obviously. In order to specify it,
I shall refer to the doctrine discussed in the previous chapter.
There I gave a short account of what led up to the council of
Nicea, at which the Christian community, reluctantly and for the
first time, added a non-scriptural word to its doctrinal vocabulary
in order to meet an emergency, the Arian crisis. Throughout the
ensuing controversy, both those who favored some variation on
Arius's teaching and those who opposed it root and branch were
agreed on one thing: the real issue was *how* Christian scripture,
particularly what it says about Christ, ought to be interpreted.
Thus Athanasius explained the bone of contention, *homoousios*,
by arguing that everything scripture says is true of the Father
it also says is true of his Son, Jesus Christ.

But does it? Athanasius's rule of thumb for understanding
the Nicene watchword implies that the New Testament's many
ways of speaking about Christ are all getting at the same thing
the bishops said, more concisely, in 325. Modern biblical scholarship, however, is inclined to take the opposite view of the New
Testament, underscoring its diversity. Not only does it belong
as a whole to a different context from the present; each of the
individual writings it comprises also belongs to a particular time
and place and point of view, a context more or less difficult
to harmonize straightforwardly with the others. Since none of

the patristic writers was a critical historian, it is not surprising that they did not interpret scripture with an eye to such differences of context. Nor, more importantly, were they concerned with the question of the historical Jesus as modern scholarship has raised it. But for just these reasons the developments in Christian doctrine for which the early fathers were responsible are now regarded by some theologians as, at best, interesting period pieces. The light of critical history exposes the unsoundness of patristic theology's largely unquestioned premise—that scripture is the bearer of a truth valid for all times—and consequently, so the argument runs, doctrines such as the one defined at Nicea must now be set aside so that Christian doctrine can be based directly on the New Testament.

There is much to be said for this argument. The big question, however, is what basing Christian doctrine directly on the New Testament amounts to in practice. If it means waiting until historical scholarship has finished discovering the Jesus of history, we shall be waiting a very long time. Meanwhile, there is a different approach, which I began to use in the previous section. It builds, not on the shifting sands of inference about the historical Jesus, but on the firmer ground of first-hand evidence, evidence we now have, evidence for the beliefs and practices of the earliest Christians as it is found in their writings. In order to develop this rather different way of relating scripture and doctrine, I propose to conduct an experiment.

My experiment can be performed only in thought, for reasons that will become clear as it proceeds, but I think it will help to illuminate the topic of this chapter. I begin with an imaginary subject, whom I shall call Elizabeth. I shall suppose that she is endowed with unlimited time, the patience of Job, and a copy of the New Testament; further, she has been addressed and transformed by the Christian message, which has oriented her living towards a mysterious, unstinting love that she knows is somehow connected with the source of the message she has thus responded to. And finally, being human, Elizabeth is someone who asks

questions. In sum, she is in very much the position I described
in the previous section, when she turns to the New Testament and
asks, 'Who is Jesus?'

The experiment begins as Elizabeth decides to concentrate
her inquiry on just one of the ways in which the New Testament
speaks about this Jesus. Her question is, 'How shall I understand
for myself who Jesus is, as *Son of God*?' That this title means
something, Elizabeth is inclined to believe, on the ground that
she trusts the early Christians by and for whom the New Testament was written to have known what they were talking about.
Still, what it does mean is a further question, since several interpretations are possible. 'Son of God' could be the kind of honor-
ific title that was often given in antiquity to persons of eminence,
rulers and the like. Alternatively, it could be the mythic language
of some other religion, borrowed by the New Testament writers.
But these are inferences that attempt to get behind the first-hand
evidence, and Elizabeth is less interested in where the title came
from than in how the early Christians used it. Is there evidence for
how they *understood* Jesus as 'Son of God'?

There is. But it is not the sort of evidence that a statistical
analysis will help Elizabeth to interpret. Take Paul, for example.
The four letters he undoubtedly wrote are the very earliest evidence for Christian belief, earlier by at least a generation than the
earliest of the gospels. 'Son of God' appears in these letters perhaps fourteen times; not many, compared with how often Paul
uses the title 'Lord.' Elizabeth, however, can do more than count.
She discovers that Paul reserves 'Son of God' for use at the climax
of important sections of his letters. In the one he wrote to the
church at Rome, the part that Luther called 'the gospel according
to Paul' is an example. Here the gist of what he says can be put
in one sentence: the Son of God makes us sons of God, as the
Spirit crying 'Abba! Father!' in us proves (Rom 8:3, 14-17,
29-32).

Paul is making a point about what Jesus has done and is
doing. As a result of the love of God shown in the death of his

Son, the love of God is poured into our hearts through the gift of the Holy Spirit (Rom 5:5, 8, 10). Accordingly, Elizabeth makes a preliminary reply to the question she began with. 'One criterion by which Jesus can be understood as Son of God,' she says to herself, 'is the experience I have of my own status as a child of God. God was in Jesus in something like the way God is in me—as Spirit, as the fulfillment of my being, as transforming, saving love.' So far so good. Elizabeth's tentative answer would be applauded by theologians who hold that Jesus was a man to whom God was fully present. But there is more evidence to be taken into account than the few passages referred to so far. Elizabeth has arrived at an understanding of Jesus as Son of God that fits well with another of Paul's statements. In his letter to the Galatian church he writes, "It is no longer I who live, but Christ who lives in me; and the life I now live in the flesh I live by faith in the Son of God, who loved me" (Gal 2:20). But what sort of life is it? At the beginning of this verse, Paul tells in two words, one of which he coined himself, why it is that he is no longer alive: he has been 'co-crucified with Christ.'

Disturbing words, these. Yet Elizabeth will not have failed to notice that Paul lays great stress on Christ's having suffered a death that was both hideous in itself and the most shameful of punishments besides. Nor is this a Pauline idiosyncracy. The New Testament is full of it. The episode of Peter's confession discussed earlier, whatever else it may be evidence for, indicates that for 'Matthew' there was no Christ without the cross. Genuinely to accept Jesus as Son of God was to accept his suffering. And in all the gospels the passion of Jesus, his arrest and trials and execution, is the center of gravity. The Gospel of Mark, earliest of the four, has aptly been called a passion story with a preface. So it is in Paul's letter to the Christians at Rome. "God shows his love for us in that while we were yet sinners Christ died for us" (5:8). "He who did not spare his own Son but gave him up for us all, will he not also give us all things with him?" (8:32). "We were reconciled to God by the death of his Son" (5:10).

What is Elizabeth to make of all this? If the Christian message is the story of a teacher, a prophet, a wholly righteous person, even 'a man to whom God was fully present,' the end of the story strikes a jarring note. Elizabeth might find herself asking whether she can really affirm with Paul that the reconciling love of God is shown in a man's death by torture. Is that the sort of thing God would do? Is it consistent with the unconditional love that Elizabeth herself knows as a matter of her own experience? Can a story that revolves around a crucifixion be a gospel, a joyful announcement of salvation? Or does the difficulty lie instead in understanding Jesus, in whose death the early Christians did find divine love displayed, as merely 'a man to whom God was fully present'? Does their calling him Son of God mean instead that he was God in person, firing the hearts of men and women by suffering and dying, drawing everyone to himself by being thus lifted up?

Elizabeth's investigation of the New Testament title 'Son of God' has led her to an issue that is equivalent to the one raised by the Arian controversy: are we saved by God, or by a creature? And that is the first point of my thought-experiment. The question which the Nicene decree answered is a meaningful question, but it raises another. Having asked a question with the same import as the question faced at Nicea, could the imaginary Elizabeth go on with her inquiry and reach an equivalent *answer*?

Let us suppose that she is ready to affirm Jesus not only as someone to whom God was present, but also as himself divine. Very well; but Tertullian and Origen both said as much. Even Arius, somewhat disingenuously, said it. Since I have deliberately confined Elizabeth's acquaintance with Christian tradition to the New Testament, she is not in a position to know about the early patristic writers. Nevertheless she is shrewd enough to figure out that it is one thing to say that Jesus is divine, that his divinity is the divinity of the God he called Father, and something else again to have a clear and unambiguous conception of divinity. If this insight were combined with a materialistic turn of mind, Elizabeth might reason that if divinity is real it must be tangible, or at least

imaginable, and that the divinity which the Son shares with his
Father must therefore be some kind of stuff. Or, finding that
this somewhat naive speculation leads her to conclude either
that there are two Gods or else that there is no real difference
between the Father and the Son, Elizabeth might abandon it,
and work out instead a notion of divinity as altogether intan-
gible and immaterial, such that the Father possesses it fully
and the Son, somehow, participates in it. Or, as a third possibility, Elizabeth might stick to scripture. She might observe
that besides 'Son of God' a number of other titles and images
are applied to Jesus, and that what is said about him in these
many and various ways is much the same as what is said about
God. She might even end up concluding that the drift of all this
is to ascribe to Jesus all the attributes of God except for the
name 'Father.'

If Elizabeth were to put this last possibility into a formula,
she would have come up with what is for all intents and purposes the 'rule of Athanasius,' and thus she would have arrived
at an answer that says what the council of Nicea said by declaring
that the Son is *homoousios* with the Father. That is the second
point of my thought-experiment. What I have intended it to
suggest is analogous to the idea that 'ontogeny recapitulates
philogeny.' The growth of an individual embryo, it was once
thought, passes sequentially through stages resembling the stages
of evolution that led to the species the embryo belongs to;
similarly, the imaginary Elizabeth, who set out to understand
for herself who Jesus is as Son of God, recapitulated in her own
investigation the sequence of stages in the development that
led to the decision taken at Nicea more than sixteen hundred
years ago—all except the term 'consubstantial.' But then, I have
pointed out already that the term never has been all that important in itself. What matters is how it is used. At Nicea it was
used as a kind of abbreviation in order to answer one quite specific
question. Elizabeth asked much the same question, and arrived
at the same answer, though not the same word. Her conclusion
about what the title 'Son of God' means is therefore no more and

no less momentous than Athanasius's explanation of the Son's consubstantiality with the Father.

My thought-experiment, then, has retraced the historical process discussed in chapter five. Elizabeth's independent discovery of what was decided at Nicea is not impossible, only improbable in the extreme—something on the order of reinventing the wheel. That is one reason why her investigation could only be imaginary. But there is another and more important reason. My thought-experiment was conducted as though there were only two separate and independent entities to be considered: Elizabeth, a set of printed pages, and nothing else. It might seem obvious that interpretation does consist in such a confrontation between a subject (the interpreter) and an object (the text to be interpreted). But what seems obvious often proves to be nothing of the sort, and interpretation is a case in point. The notion that it is basically a confrontation can take either of two conflicting forms, both mistaken.

On one hand there is the view that the meaning of a text can always be determined, because it is just *there*, lying plainly in view. Readers who do not see this meaning must have their eyes closed, and readers who substitute some other meaning are deliberately being perverse. Interpretation is, quite simply, a matter of reading out of the text what is already in it. Where this view locates meaning in the text, the opposite view locates it in the interpreter. The meaning, that is, consists wholly in the reader's response to the text, and meaning is produced anew every time there is a confrontation between text and interpreter. Interpretation is a matter of reading into texts whatever the reader chooses. They are the stage on which any number of mental ballets can be performed.

These alternatives are variations on a theme that has turned up several times before, the theme of subjects and objects as fixed and immutable entities, one of which has got to take logical priority. But the dilemma of deciding which is prior is a purely logical beast, which can thrive only in a static environment. In the real world, the world of human meaning, neither subjects nor objects are static, and so the dilemma becomes a red herring It is quite true that readers 'make' meanings, as the second view of interpretation mentioned above insists. Texts do not think or suppose, consider or decide or feel. Human beings do. By doing it, they mean something, and by meaning something they change themselves. Meaning 'makes' readers and readers 'make' meanings at one and the same time. Interpreting a text is not a confrontation. It is a doubly creative act of meaning. And it never takes place in the kind of vacuum I dreamed up for Elizabeth to do her interpreting in; that is the main reason why I could only conduct my thought-experiment in thought. Every actual interpretation builds in some way on previous interpretations. This is obviously true in the case of interpretations that simply repeat what everyone else has said and add a few footnotes. Even a fresh and original interpretation, however, is either a rebuttal of previous views, or an adjustment of them, or a synthesis, or an expansion.

What I am suggesting about interpretation in general follows from what I have already said about community and history, and it applies right across the board. If you want to do more than pass your eyes over the pages of, say, the *Divine Comedy*, and you are not already a member of some community that has some tradition of interpreting Dante, you will have to find your way into one. The same goes, in different ways, for any profound text. It goes for the New Testament especially.

Like other texts, the New Testament is susceptible of various kinds of interpretation, and so there are several overlapping communities that interpret it. Historians of language interpret the text as evidence for Greek prose syntax in the first century; historians of antiquity, as evidence for certain aspects of life in one province of the Roman empire; historians of religion, as one of several pieces of evidence for the origins of Christianity. But as 'saving history,' as an account of what salvation is and why it happens, as evidence for what God has done in Christ, as a book that is not just about a particular religion but also part of it, the New Testament has its meaning in and for another community of interpretation, that is, the church.

5

Is the doctrine that Jesus Christ is truly God, consubstantial with the Father, in the New Testament? That depends on what is meant by 'in the New Testament.' I have suggested just now that nothing is 'in' the New Testament in quite the same way Anchorage is in Alaska. What is in a text, spatially speaking, is a lot of black marks on paper. The question is what they mean. But here again the metaphor misleads. 'They,' the marks, are only potentially meaningful. Meaning is an act; it depends on human agency. And if human agency gets into the act of meaning, so does everything that makes human beings human—what they already understand, where they learned it, how it was taught to them, and much more. That is why I ended the previous section by dismissing the idea that interpreting is like the collision of isolated billiard balls in empty space. It is, rather, an ongoing process, a community enterprise.

In particular, interpreting the Bible is part of the process through which Christian community constitutes itself. In its cooperative effort, over time, to understand its own tradition, more especially the privileged component of that tradition which it calls the New Testament, the church is continually bringing itself into being. In that sense, it is Christian scripture that has made, and is still making, the church. But conversely the church has made, and is still making, its scripture. The reason is the same in both cases: interpretation consists in the activities that define both interpreters and the meaning of what they interpret. Two examples of this process will help to show how it goes on in the Christian community.

First, what is a poem? There are any number of verbal definitions, the sort that a dictionary might provide, but none of them applies to everything that can be thought of as poetry and to nothing else. One notable literary critic, Stanley Fish, has suggested why such definitions are bound to fail. It is because almost any set of words *can* be understood as poetry. By way of example, Fish tells of arriving at the room in which he was to teach a class on modern poetry and finding that a list of surnames had been left on the blackboard after some earlier class. He let this list stand, and found that his students were quite capable of deriving from it a variety of poetic meanings. By exercising their interpretive skill, they 'made' the list a poem. Does that mean that the question of what counts as poetry admits of as many answers as there are individuals who ask it? More generally, was Humpty Dumpty right when he solemnly informed Alice that when *he* used a word it meant just what he chose it to mean, neither more nor less?

Not entirely, Fish replies. What can be interpreted as poetry and what cannot does depend on decision, but it does not follow that literary criticism is a free-for-all. Interpreting is an activity that has to be learned, and by learning it one enters a community for which not every combination of words is a poem and not every interpretation is an acceptable one. There are standards, in other words, but they do not exist outside communities of literary criticism. Hence agreement is quite possible, but only within some interpretive tradition that continually defines and redefines both what literature is and what it is to be a literary critic. Those who share the same values and thus belong to the same community can judge the correctness of an interpretation, though the criteria for judgment may change when the community does.

My second example of interpretation as a creative enterprise is adjudication, "the process by which a judge comes to understand and express the meaning of an authoritative legal text and the values embodied in that text." In order to analyze what this process entails, legal philosopher Owen M. Fiss refers to an issue in constitutional law. There is no specific directive in the Constitution about how students shall be assigned to public schools; there is only the general provision that no state shall 'deny to any person within its jurisdiction the equal protection of the laws.' What is meant by 'state,' 'person,' 'jurisdiction,' 'protection,' 'laws,' or—a notoriously difficult term—'equal'? In each case it is a question of interpretation. But Fiss argues that there is more to answering such questions than a judge's imposition, Humpty-Dumpty-like, of his or her own meaning. There are rules for legal interpretation, and these rules "are not simply standards or principles held by individual judges, but instead constitute the institution (the profession) in which judges find themselves and through which they act." Nor do judges belong to this interpretive community, as literary critics belong to theirs, simply because they happen to share certain views. They belong because they are committed to upholding and advancing the rule of law itself; committed, that is, to interpreting legal texts as prescriptive.

Accordingly, the procedures that define adjudication require that judges must be independent of the interests of the parties in a given case; they must listen to all parties that will be directly affected by the decision; and they must justify their rulings in generally applicable terms. These procedural constraints, in other words, define not only adjudication in general but also the correctness of any particular interpretation of the law. By setting limits on how adjudication proceeds, they define both the community of jurisprudence and what the law *is*. For, except in a purely formal sense, the printed text as it appears 'on the books' is not the law. It might be just a dead letter. Nor is the law simply what the legislators who passed it intended. What a given law meant at the time it was framed is part of what it means thereafter, but times change, and the need for adjudication arises because they do. The questions that come up in new situations often go far beyond anything the original framers had in mind. And, in turn, each new answer adds to what the law means.

Decisions as to what counts as poetry and what poetry means are also decisions that make the community of literary criticism; so too decisions as to what counts as law and what the law means are decisions that make the community of adjudication. Both are processes that control the meaning conveyed by texts. Similarly, decisions as to what counts as scripture and what that scripture means are decisions that make the church. Even the imaginary Elizabeth in my thought-experiment was not entirely independent of the church, as an interpretive community, when she set out to understand Jesus as Son of God. She was interpreting texts that came to her as a collection, not piecemeal, and the collecting was done by the Christian community when it 'canonized' the books of the New Testament. The process of deciding that these texts, and only these, should inform Christian worship and witness was a complicated one, and many of its details are not altogether clear to historians. What is clear, however, is that by defining which writings should count as its scriptures, the church was defining itself as (among other things) that community which lives by the meanings those writings convey.

Moreover, the emergence of the scriptural canon helped to define what those meanings are. By drawing a line between what was scripture and what was not, it also put each of the canonized texts into an interpretive context. Thus each of the four canonical gospels has been interpreted in light of the others. The process of interpretation would have been different if any of the four had been omitted from the canon, and very different if any of the non-canonical gospels, of which there are several, had been included. Similarly, the whole New Testament has been interpreted in light of the writings that Christians call the Old Testament, and would have been interpreted quite differently if the church had decided to exclude them. This is not to say that having a relatively stable collection of texts wholly determines what any of them means. The canon is only a formal context of interpretation: it defines what it is important for the church to understand. In that sense, scripture is its own interpreter—but not in the sense that it has answers to all the questions it raises.

As with the Constitution, changing circumstances generate questions which cannot be resolved in the terms that are used in the text itself.

To put it another way, the text of scripture is normative because it functions that way, not simply because it is 'on the books.' The Bible becomes normative for the common life of Christians in so far as they appeal to it, interpret it, and apply its meaning to concrete questions. All of this is part of the ongoing, historical process that *is* Christian community, and it is why the Bible *is* scripture and not just a sampling of ancient Near Eastern literature. Conversely, to the extent that some book or passage is not so used—the Epistle of James, perhaps, or Paul's exhortations on the behavior of women—it reverts to dead-letter status. In fact, what is called the 'functional canon,' the parts of scripture used *as* scripture, has almost always been narrower than the formal canon. Not everything the formal canon contains has been equally important, for the very good reason that importance is not a quality that inheres in texts, like the color of the ink or the shape of the letters. What is important about any text, the Bible included, depends on the questions that are put to it, and it is through a cumulative, self-correcting process of raising and answering questions about the meaning of the Bible that the Bible has had its importance for nineteen centuries and more of Christian living. The normative meaning of Christian scripture will be completely determined when all the relevant questions have been raised and put to rest, and not before, because then and only then will there be a closed, permanent context in which its meaning can be completely understood. Meanwhile, the process goes on.

The process goes on, and it is the process itself, the raising and answering of successive questions, that bridges the gap between the centuries. I have said a good deal about the problem of the New Testament's 'pastness,' its temporal distance from modern ways of thinking, but there is one way in which this remoteness is not so much a problem as an asset. It is a commonplace adage that the real significance of events appears only in retrospect. So it was only after Augustine the grown man had been converted under the fig-tree that he came to see what it meant that Augustine the boy had robbed a pear-tree. So too it will be years before the significance of the Vietnam war can be seen in perspective. And so also with the events to which the New Testament bears witness. Their effects are still being realized, in both senses of the word—understood, comprehended, and also brought about. As Krister Stendahl has put it, the bridge between what the New Testament meant, and what it now means, is to be found "in the actual history of the church as still ongoing sacred history of God's people." What God has done in Christ he has done unrepeatably, once for all, but it has not been "frozen and canned in the canon." The 'sacred history' of what he has done continues. The church's decision about what would count as its scripture was no arbitrary choice. It was a corporate act of discernment, made under the impact of the same events that had brought the church into existence in the first place.

The consolidation of the Christian Bible did two things. First, it set formal boundaries on interpretation. It designated the privileged expressions of the Christian message, the 'charter documents' that the church, as a community of interpretation, has to interpret. But secondly, the decision about what counts as scripture was also a decision about what the Christian message of salvation means. Specifically, it does not mean that Christ as savior was the bearer of an esoteric wisdom which released the enlightened from their enslavement to a material world created by a perverse and subordinate god. Those who preached this doctrine claimed that it had been privately handed down to them from Jesus himself. They were ruled out of bounds by ruling in writings which were public and which identified the God whom Jesus called Father with the Creator who "saw everything that he had made, and behold, it was very good" (Gen 1:31). At one and the same time, the Christian community was defining both itself and its common meaning. The same thing happened later, when the Arians claimed that their view of salvation had the backing of canonical scripture. The council of Nicea ruled them out by ruling in the interpretation of Christ as savior that I have discussed in the previous chapter. Here too the church, by regulating the interpretation of scripture, was defining both itself and its common meaning.

The answer that Nicea gave to the question of who Christ is raised others—whether the Holy Spirit too was consubstantial with the Father; whether one and the same Christ was born of Mary as well as 'eternally begotten of the Father'; whether he is fully human as well as fully divine. All of these questions were answered at church councils. Taken together, the answers express the mind of the Christian community, the ongoing context in which the church clarified its message. The conciliar doctrines regulate what the Christian community *says* about the source of its salvation, by means of propositions *about* what it says. By entering a context that was logical in the sense I outlined in chapter five, the church did not leave behind the rich, symbolic language of its scriptures or clip the wings of their soaring imagery. It did, however, decline to take the Humpty Dumpty view of language. What the Christian word means is not just what anybody chooses it to mean. Within the community of interpretation, there are restraints, broad but definite, on what counts as an acceptable way of talking about the Christ set forth in the New Testament.

At Nicea, I have argued, this community turned a corner. The church accepted a logical technique, one small part of the Greek 'discovery of mind,' and used it to state in a new and precise way it meant when it proclaimed Christ as Son of God. Accepting scholarly techniques, part of the heritage of the modern discovery of human historicity, will have been no less momentous a turning point—'will have been,' because historical scholarship is taking even longer to get used to than the *homoousios* did. To enter this still fuller context is not to abandon the logical context of the early councils, any more than the councils themselves abandoned the imaginative context of the Bible. It is to ask questions that could not have been asked before the rise of modern scholarship. By answering them, the church is becoming aware that it is not a permanent resident in the 'house of authority' but an ongoing, historical community of interpretation.

The idea that such a community should set aside all its previous interpretations, in order to start afresh on the raw data of the New Testament, is rather like the idea that you can set aside your adolescence in order to start your life afresh with innocent infancy. Such a feat would amount to setting aside yourself, since the 'you' who would be performing it would *be* 'you' only because of a particular history, the whole sequence of decisions you had made since infancy. Every person is what he or she has become. So is every community. And the church is what it is because it has defined itself through a particular historical series of interpretive decisions. Acknowledging one's personal past need not be smug or uncritical; nor is anyone simply locked into the patterns set by past decisions. Similarly, it need not be triumphalism to acknowledge the ongoing process that has made the church what it is. Not every question raised about the Christian message has been answered intelligently, reasonably, lovingly. There have been derailments, detours, and still unresolved doctrinal quarrels, and these too are part of what the Christian community now is. But the way to undo the mischief is not to abandon ship. It is to change course. And the way to do that is to know the route that has been taken so far.

That is why the work of New Testament scholars has a particularly important part to play in the life of the Christian community: they map the starting point (in so far as there is first-hand evidence for it) of the trajectory the church has followed in interpreting the message it lives by. What that message *meant*, how Paul or any of the other New Testament writers understood it, did not determine for all time what it would mean. But knowing what it did mean gives the church a landmark from which to take its bearings.

Yet locating the landmarks is not enough. There is a further question. I have referred to Stendahl's suggestion that there is a link between what the Bible has meant and what it means today if the factual history of interpretation, the route that the Christian community has actually taken, is part of the still ongoing sacred history of God's people. Is it? Has the trajectory been the right trajectory? That is exactly the same kind of question as whether the New Testament writers themselves had the right idea about Jesus to begin with, and such questions cannot be answered by intelligence alone. They call for discernment, for the eye of faith, as well. In the end they are asking whether God's people have been godly, whether Paul or Athanasius or the most recent biblical commentator has understood what is consistent with almighty love, whether the promise of a Spirit who will lead into all truth has been kept.

Put that way, the question is one that it seems presumptuous to answer. Yet answered it must be. God either enters the world of human meaning, speaks a saving word in history, discloses his love in Christ—the whole Christ, head and members—or he does not.

❧ SEVEN ☙

Do Doctrines Matter?

Whatsoever God doth work, the hands of all three persons are jointly and equally in it . . . The Father as goodness, the Son as wisdom, the Holy Ghost as power do all concur in every particular outwardly issuing from that one only glorious deity which they all are.

RICHARD HOOKER

WHEN I FIRST began to work on it, this book already existed. It existed as an idea. I do not mean that I had a mental blueprint, complete in every detail, showing how the finished product should turn out. I had nothing of the sort. Nor do I mean anything deep or mystical or philosophical by 'idea.' All I mean is that something had happened, the kind of thing pictured in cartoons as a lightbulb flashing on over someone's head. There is a conscious click as the tumblers fall into place. The light dawns. You are 'on to' something. You get the point—exactly what point, you have to find out. In my case, the book was finished; all I had to do was write it. Everything was there, complete, 'the end in the beginning,' though until I was almost done writing I could not say very cogently (as my editor will attest) what my idea was or what the book was going to be about. I knew all along what I would be saying, yet until it was said I did not really know what I knew. The introductory chapter was the last to be written, because it was only when I had put the next five chapters on paper that I realized what there was to introduce.

There is nothing especially mystifying about this. Certainly it is not unique to writers. As the lady quoted in E.M. Forster puts it, 'How can I know what I think till I see what I say?' All of us

have had the experience of being at a loss for words, of having
the expression we want on the tip of our tongue, or of not knowing our own mind on some question. The idea is there, but it has
yet to be embodied in words so that we can recognize it, reflect
on it, and know what we have understood. Writing a book, to
judge from my own experience, is a long drawn-out process of
knowing what I think by seeing what I say. All the various activities that make up the craft of authorship, everything from
outlining chapters to weighing the relative merits of words that
are nearly synonymous, are aspects of the slow metamorphosis
through which an idea turns into a book. It is these activities
that are most evident to the author, whether they take place
mentally or, as they usually do in my case, along with the physical
activity of spreading ink on paper. And since they provide the
verbal shape without which even the brightest idea would remain
vague and indefinite, it seems logical to suppose that the idea
depends on them for its existence. The making of books is
proverbially endless, but the number of books that have never
been written, because their authors never got around to the
largely uninspiring labor of fleshing out their ideas in prose,
must be enormous.

But the writing of a book is not a logical process. No creative
act is. The fact of the matter is that even when a writer's attention is wholly occupied with words, the idea is still in charge.
No doubt there are authors who write solely for the sake of seeing
their own words in print. As a rule, though, they have something
to say, and in principle all the techniques of spelling, grammar,
diction, logic, and rhetoric have as their one and only aim communicating what that something is. In other words, the craft of
wordsmithing exists for the sake of sharing ideas. Ideally, the
whole of a book and all of its particulars should conform perfectly
with the idea it embodies. To be 'right,' a turn of phrase must
not only be syntactically correct. It has to fit. The words that say
exactly what I mean may bubble up effortlessly from who knows
where; they may be the result of a hundred experiments of which
ninety-nine were failures. I may not know what I mean until I

have got them, yet when I do hit on the right expression there is a kind of inevitability about it. 'Of course! So *that* is what I wanted to say.' When it does happen, no other words will do. And the judgment that anything else would somehow sound wrong is not simply an intellectual judgment. It is personal.

I offer the preceding paragraphs, not as an embryonic theory of literary creativity but as a first-hand account of what I find myself doing as an author. As I have described it, the making of a book is a single action that takes place in three distinct activities. The first I have called getting an idea. It *is* the book, form and content, whole and parts. The light dawns; unless it does words would be meaningless markings or insignificant sound and fury. And it goes on dawning until the book has been written. The writing itself, the craft or technique of using language to make meaning articulate, is the second activity. From the author's point of view it is the most conspicuous one. It too *is* the book, more specifically, the book as a communication. Only by communicating it to myself, finding out what I mean, knowing my own mind, do I become aware of what my idea is all about. When the light dawns, it dawns in language. There was never a moment when my idea was not, as it were, expressing itself.

Yet even an excellent expression of a really good idea does not communicate anything unless someone responds to it. A book is not a book until it is read. From the reader's standpoint, the reading *is* the book, but for the author it is also a third activity in the act of making. Like the other two, it goes on constantly from the first, though for me it is most prominent when the type has been set and I am correcting the proofs. Now that my idea is embodied, literally, I become the reader of my own book and become aware of my feelings about it. Was it, I ask (now that I know what it was), a good idea? Was this (now that I can see it in black and white) the best way to express it? Does the whole thing make sense, hang together, stand on its own? Yes—sometimes, at least. Admittedly there are passages I wince at, places where for one reason or another I have failed to

say what I meant, and reading them makes me want to bury the
whole book quietly and pretend I never wrote it. But there are
also places that I love, not just because I wrote them but because
they ought to have been written; because I have said something worth saying and said it well. My response is an urge to
collar the nearest bystander and shout, 'Here—just read *that*.
You'll love it too!'

As I suggested earlier, what goes into literary creativeness is
nothing very mystifying, though some authors would like to think
so. At bottom authorship is a special case of what we all do as
members of the only biological species that makes things. Not
everyone is a creative artist in the narrower sense of making
pictures or poems, but we are all, in ways discussed at length in
chapter three, makers of ourselves. Every construction of the
human spirit, every marriage and every philosophy, every society
and institution and science, is essentially a work of art. Not all
of them are beautiful, that is, true and good. But they should be.
The same goes for the human story of which each of us is turning
out one unique and irreplaceable edition. Making oneself is like
making a piece of prose. As the idea of a book comes into being
in and as the words that convey it to a reader, so the idea we have
of ourselves and our world, our personal character and the
character of our civilization, comes into being in and as the actions
in which we express ourselves and through which we affect the
being of others. And in that sense human creativity is the most
mysterious thing in the world, for it mirrors the mystery of God.

The mind of every maker, the maker of literature or of a life,
is a reflection of the mind of the Maker. That is the title of a
remarkable book by Dorothy L. Sayers to which I am much
indebted here. Sayers uses her own terminology, but her account
of how a book is conceived and born is basically the same as the
one I have presented. From an idea there proceeds an expression,
a word of communication, which conveys the idea both to its
author and to other readers and evokes in them a response. The
maker of literature performs one conscious act in three activities,

just as the Maker of heaven and earth, according to Christian doctrine, is one God in three persons. The threefold structure of human creativity is analogous to the threefold being of the Creator.

Only God, properly speaking, creates. Even the most original author has to make use of a language that already exists, as painters have to start with pigments they did not invent. God needs nothing to work on. He creates *ex nihilo*, and as I pointed out in chapter five, this thoroughgoing distinction between Creator and creature is part of what Christians have meant since the fourth century by saying that God is God. Yet along with this distinction Christianity affirms a similarity: man, male and female, is created 'after the likeness' or 'in the image' of God. How these phrases were understood by whoever wrote the first chapter of Genesis is anybody's guess, but it is worth noting that when they appear only one assertion has been made about God. He creates. "The characteristic common to God and man," Sayers writes, "is apparently that: the desire and the ability to make things."

What the nature of human creativity *proves* about the nature of God is exactly nothing. I cannot say that too strongly. The doctrine of the Trinity cannot be read out of the workings of the human mind; it is founded on affirmations that belong to the Christian story. Raising and answering questions about that story, not psychological introspection, led the church to assert that 'that which we believe of the glory of the Father, the same we believe of the Son, and of the Holy Ghost, without any difference or inequality.' At the same time, however, *if* this assertion is true, then an image of the mind of the Maker is just what we should expect to find reflected in the minds of the makers he has made. And while the fact that we do find such an analogy does not by itself establish the doctrine of the Trinity, the analogy once it is found can provide a way of understanding what the doctrine means.

Analogies are always imperfect and potentially misleading, but when it comes to understanding God there is no alternative. For it is one thing to believe and affirm that there is one God yet three who are God, and something else to understand what one is thus affirming. If the very notion of trinity-in-unity were unthinkable, like the concept of circular squareness, Christianity's doctrine of God would be like the six impossible things that the White Queen in *Alice* claimed she could believe before breakfast. Some Christians, it is true, have insisted that the Trinity, like the other Christian mysteries properly so called, is totally unintelligible to merely human minds. By and large, however, *credo quia absurdum*, 'I believe *because* it is absurd,' has not been the church's attitude. Loving God is no doubt better than learnedly discoursing upon the Trinity. Still, as Augustine asks, "How *can* we love, by believing, that Trinity which we do not know? . . . The question is, from what likeness or comparison of known things can we believe in order that we may love God?"

He answers that although we have yet to see God face to face we can nevertheless reach some understanding of what we believe about him, because our limited acts of knowing and loving bear some resemblance to the unlimited Act who is Father, Son, and Holy Spirit. Since human consciousness is the only non-material reality we know about, Augustine follows Origen in arguing that the best analogy for God, who is utterly non-material, is a psychological analogy. Specifically, he finds a human image of the Trinity in "the mind, and the knowledge whereby the mind knows itself, and the love whereby it loves both itself and its knowledge of itself." To apply the analogy, God knows his own mind—that is, he knows himself—and this perfect self-understanding is a Word, God the Son. In us, expressing ideas takes time, but in God, the Son is 'eternally begotten of the Father.' Moreover, God loves himself, both as one who understands and as the Word of his own understanding. His loving response, his listening to the Word who is himself, is God the Spirit who 'proceeds from the Father and the Son.'

And this triune act of understanding love overflows: that is what creates the universe. Here too there is an analogy with

human creativity. It might seem that God needs to create, that
he depends on his creation in the same way a poet needs and
depends on written poetry. In fact, as Sayers observes, a poet
does nothing of the kind. Writing a poem is "an act of love
towards the poet's own imaginative act and towards his fellow-
beings. It is a social act; but the poet is, first and foremost, his
own society." So is God. The Trinity is the perfect society.
As a poet deprived of paper and ink would be no less a poet,
so God would be no less God without the universe he freely
calls into being. He creates,

> *Not to increase His good, which cannot be,*
> *But that His splendour, shining back, might say:*
> Behold, I am, *in His eternity.*

Dante's lines give voice to a doctrine of creation which implies
that every being, 'all that is, seen and unseen,' expresses the
being of God. There was once a cartoon that showed an astonished
couple gazing upwards as the sky burst open to display a dazzling
banner inscribed, 'And now, a word from our Creator.' But the
whole universe, on the Christian hypothesis, is exactly that—a
word from the Creator. Everything that has been unfolding
through the aeons is a drama, which is still being produced. Its
characters are men and women; its story-line, human history.
As an author uses marks on paper to communicate an idea, God
uses the cosmos to tell us what is on his mind.

If the meaning of the drama he is writing seems at times to
be something less than what we might expect from an infinitely
loving playwright, that is largely because we the actors consistently muff our lines. Having been delegated to create, as we are
created, in the image of God, we choose not to create, not to
understand, not to love. God makes us free not only to make
ourselves and our world but also to mar what we make, and
whatever else the Eden story may mean it suggests that the
absurdity of exercising this latter freedom is a failure on the part
of the makers, not the Maker.

This is where the other cardinal doctrine of Christianity comes in. To continue the metaphor of authorship, everything an author writes is in some way a self-disclosure. But if we want to understand an author's *omnia opera* or collected works as a whole, it will usually help if among them there is an autobiography. An autobiography 'is' its author, more than other works are, in the sense of being the fullest literary expression of the personal identity that produced the others and is, therefore, a key to interpreting them all. At the same time, though, an autobiography in itself is still a book. However faithfully it discloses its author's mind, it does so in a way that is necessarily finite. Although the 'idea' that an autobiography embodies in words is the author's self-understanding, even a perfect expression by a perfectly candid author would still be subject to the limitations of the printed page. The writing of each of the other books would have a place, within the overall pattern of the narrative, as an event in the author's life, yet the autobiography itself would also have a place, a unique one but only one, within the overall pattern of the author's *oeuvre*. It would explain how and why the others were written; it would also have to be read in the context they provide.

As the reader will probably have surmised, I am referring to the Incarnation. To say that the Word became flesh is to say that God's understanding of himself, through which he created all things—his *omnia opera*, as it were—has also been embodied in the finite deeds and words and sufferings of a single human life. How one and the same person can be what Christian doctrine says that Christ is, truly God and truly man, is far more difficult to conceive than how an autobiography can be the self-understanding of an author and still be a book. It can be done; doing it is one of the things that theology is for. I am, however, more concerned here with what the doctrine of the Incarnation implies. For if it is true that the whole course of history is a word being spoken by God, it would follow that every person and every event, everything that has happened, is happening, and will happen, means something as part of a single drama composed by a single mind. God himself 'gets the point' of the universe; that is why it exists. By thinking it, he causes it to be. But we, the characters enacting the drama, have to take our individual and corporate parts in it with only a very imperfect grasp of what it all means. Faith, in the sense discussed in chapter two, is the assurance that there *is* a point, a meaning to be grasped. Yet how can we understand what that meaning is? The drama is not over. We can neither consult the script directly nor leave the stage and become spectators. It is hard enough to find rhyme or reason in our personal lives, let alone intelligibility in the whole pageant of world history.

There is, however, one particular episode in the human drama to which Christianity would call everyone's attention; an episode, to quote Sayers again, in which the leading part was played

> by the Author, who presents it as a brief epitome of the plan of the whole work. If we ask, "What *kind* of play is this that we are acting?" the answer put forward is: "Well, it is *this* kind of play." And examining the plot of it, we observe at once that if anybody in this play has his feelings spared, it is certainly not the Author.

The doctrine of the Trinity declares that the *why* of all things is infinite, understanding Love; the doctrine of the Incarnation, that this Love can be loved. What does it look like, the loving Word that the Creator speaks in all that is? It looks like a cross. How does almighty Love respond to the lovelessness of his own creatures? Not by exercising any force that would overrule their freedom, if the plot of the Christian story is any clue; nor by dispensing a justice that would give them their deserts. He responded with self-sacrifice.

If that is the point of the 'brief epitome' personally enacted by the Author, then it is also the point of all his other works. God utters only one word, the Word who is himself. In that sense the Christian story is nothing less than an explanation of who we are, where we are going, and how we get there. It is nothing less, but it is more. By disclosing the Creator it invites us to create. To decide for this story is to decide for the universe, and to decide for the person whose story it is, the carpenter who was crucified, is to decide for the God in whom we live and move and have our being.

And here my book returns to its starting point, for such a decision is itself a gift. The values expounded in the gospel are not obvious and never have been. When Nietzsche wrote, "*God on the cross*—are the horrible secret thoughts behind this symbol not understood yet? All that suffers, all that is nailed to the cross, is *divine*," he meant it as an exclamation of disgust and scorn. But he was, and knew that he was, close to the heart of Christian doctrine. No one has recognized more penetratingly that the problem of being human and the problem of creativity are one and the same. To *be*, in the fullest and most personal sense, is to create. The only question is how. What is it that lets something new loose in the world—the act of autonomous power or the act of self-surrender? In the long run there is no third answer. If you try to have it both ways, one of them will always end up assimilating the other. You will either redefine self-surrender to mean Dionysian abandon, or else redefine power to mean that which is made perfect in weakness.

That the second of these is the principle of creation, as God understands it, is the word that has entered the human world of meaning in Christ. "And by Him is illuminated the time in which we execute those choices through which our freedom is realized or prevented, for the course of History is predictable in the degree to which all men love themselves, and spontaneous in the degree to which each man loves God and through Him his neighbour." Of that sentence, spoken by Simeon in Auden's "For the Time Being," Christian doctrine—the Incarnation, the Trinity, and everything else the church believes, teaches, and confesses on the basis of the word of God—is an explication. Do these doctrines matter?

If it matters what we make of ourselves and our world; if it matters how we weave the social, institutional, political, economic fabric of our lives; if it matters whether we, like God, are persons; if, in sum, the question to which they are Christianity's answer is an important question, then, possibly, Christian doctrines matter. They propose that the question itself, our search for our humanity, is the prompting of a Spirit whose work in the world is to draw our restless hearts, through a Word who makes all things new, to a Father whose will is our peace. As it stands, that is just a pious saying. As it has been lived for two thousand years by all sorts and conditions of men and women, it is the only truth worth knowing.

APPENDIX

The Creed of the Council of Nicea
19 June 325

We believe in one God,
 the Father, the Almighty,
 maker of all that is, seen and unseen.

We believe in one Lord, Jesus Christ,
 the Son of God,
 begotten of the Father as Only-begotten,
 that is, from the substance of the Father,
 God from God, Light from Light,
 true God from true God,
 begotten, not made,
 of one Being [*homoousios*] with the Father.
 Through him all things were made,
  things in heaven and things on earth.
 For us and for our salvation he came down:
  he became incarnate and was made man and suffered.
  On the third day he rose again;
  he ascended into heaven.
 He will come again to judge the living and the dead.

We believe in the Holy Spirit.

But as for those who say, 'There was when he was not,'
 or 'Before he was begotten, he was not,'
 or 'He was made out of nothing';
 or who affirm that the Son of God is of a different subsistence or substance, or a creature, or mutable, or subject to change—
 these the catholic and apostolic church denounces and cuts off.

The Council of Chalcedon's
'Definition of the Faith'
22 October 451

Therefore, following the holy fathers, we are united in teaching all to acknowledge:

one and the same Son, our Lord Jesus Christ,
the same, complete in divinity, and the same, complete in humanity,
truly God and truly man,
    consisting also of a reasonable soul and body,
the same, of one substance [*homoousios*] with the Father
    as regards his divinity,
and the same, of one substance with us
    as regards his humanity;
like us in all respects except for sin;
as regards his divinity,
    begotten of the Father before all worlds,
but yet, as regards his humanity,
    begotten for us and for our salvation of Mary the Virgin, the God-bearer;
one and the same Christ, Son, Lord, Only-begotten,
recognized in two natures,
    without confusion, without change, without division,
    without separation;
    the distinction of natures being in no way annulled by the union, but rather the characteristics of each nature being preserved and coming together to form one person and subsistence,
not as parted or separated into two persons,
but one and the same Son and Only-begotten God the Word,
    Lord Jesus Christ,
even as the prophets from earliest times spoke of him,
and our Lord Jesus Christ himself taught us,
and the creed of the fathers handed down to us.

SOURCES

CHAPTER ONE

1 Epigraph. Joseph Butler, *The Analogy of Religion* (1736).

"prolegomena . . . . passengers?" Helmut Thielicke, *The Ethics of Sex*, trans. John W. Doberstein (New York: Harper & Row, 1964), p. v.

3 "to understand . . . it." Aristotle, *Posterior Analytics* 90a 31.

5 "It is a lie. . . . realism." Dorothy L. Sayers, "Creed or Chaos?" in *Christian Letters to a Post-Christian World* (Grand Rapids, MI: William B. Eerdmans, 1969), p. 31.

7 "an inward. . . heart." Butler, *Analogy.*

CHAPTER TWO

11 Epigraph. William Law, *The Spirit of Love* (1752).

15 "When my girl's. . . . said!" Quoted by Dorothy L. Sayers, "Dante and Charles Williams" in *Christian Letters*, p. 163.

"The quality. . . guilt." Charles Williams, *The Figure of Beatrice* (London: Faber & Faber, 1943), p. 37.

16 "Capacities . . . used." Abraham H. Maslow, *Toward a Psychology of Being*, 2d ed. (New York: Van Nostrand Reinhold Co., 1968), p. 201.

"become. . . perfection." Maslow, p. 95.

"at one particular. . . . get it again." C.S. Lewis, *That Hideous Strength* (New York: Macmillan, 1965), pp. 318-19.

19 "So impressive. . . blind." Maslow, p. 43.

"You talk as if life were good." Charles Williams, *Descent Into Hell* (Grand Rapids, MI: William B. Eerdmans, 1949), p. 95.

20 "revealed to us. . . embraces." Austin Farrer, *Love Almighty and Ills Unlimited* (New York: Doubleday & Co., 1961), p. 162.

21   "the fearsome... evil." Hannah Arendt, *Eichmann in Jerusalem,* rev. ed. (New York: Penguin Books, 1977).

22   "Faith.... self-forgetting charity." Wilfred Cantwell Smith, *Belief and History* (Charlottesville, VA: University Press of Virginia, 1977), p. 93.

     "to have faith... thing." H. Richard Niebuhr, *Radical Monotheism and Western Culture* (New York: Harper & Row, 1970), p. 119.

23   "One's faith... century." Smith, p. 96.

27   "God is.... class of people?" Austin Farrer, "Revelation," in Basil Mitchell, ed., *Faith and Logic* (London: George Allen & Unwin, 1957), p. 97.

33   "I am the man.... they were not mine." G.K. Chesterton, *Orthodoxy* (New York: Doubleday & Co., 1959), pp. 11-12.

34   "There was.... seeds of doctrine." Chesterton, p. 65.

     "things that.... learnt it." Chesterton, p. 12.

35   *Whether at once... skill....* Gerard Manley Hopkins, "The Wreck of the Deutschland."

CHAPTER THREE

37   Epigraph. Charles Williams, *He Came Down From Heaven* (London: William Heinemann, 1938), p. 25.

41   *A serious house... destinies.* Philip Larkin, "Church Going," *The Less Deceived* (New York: St. Martin's Press, 1960), p. 29.

43   "You tell... 'pinions is." Mark Twain, "Corn-Pone Opinions," *Europe and Beyond.*

48   "a titanic... past." Edward Shils, *Tradition* (Chicago: University of Chicago Press, 1981), p. 197.

51   "a present... future things." Augustine, *Confessions* 11. 20.

54   "The distinction... conceive." C.S. Lewis, *Surprised by Joy* (New York: Harcourt Brace Jovanovich, 1955), pp. 192-3.

58 "without God... way of life." Dwight D. Eisenhower, 1955, quoted in Will Herberg, *Protestant–Catholic–Jew* (New York: Doubleday & Co., 1955), pp. 274-5.

"American... the other." Herberg, p. 15.

60 "The very... other." Sebastian Moore, *The Inner Loneliness* (New York: The Crossroad Publishing Co., 1982), p. 14.

"Now one.... other persons." Moore, p. 13.

64 "an educational... explosions." Rosemary Haughton, *The Transformation of Man* (Springfield, IL: Templegate Publishers, 1980), p. 155; see also p. 150.

"religion... purposes." Haughton, p. 247.

65 "What the church... doctrine." Jaroslav Pelikan, *The Christian Tradition: A History of the Development of Doctrine*, vol. 1 (Chicago: University of Chicago Press, 1971), p. 1.

66 "Grace is... our wills." From the Catechism, *The Book of Common Prayer* (1979).

CHAPTER FOUR

71 Epigraph. C.S. Lewis, *The Allegory of Love* (Oxford: Oxford University Press, 1936), p. 1.

76 "are no more... health." Austin Farrer, "Revelation," p. 88.

He that... still. Samuel Butler, *Hudibras.*

77 *quod... omnibus.* Vincent of Lérins, *Commonitorium* 2.3.

81 "as this means... salvation." Thomas Aquinas, *Summa Theologiae*, foreword to part 3. For what follows, see part 3, question 2, article 1.

86 "has been referred... room." Edward Farley, *Ecclesial Reflection* (Philadelphia: Fortress Press, 1982), p. 166. I should point out that while my diagram takes its inspiration from one of Farley's examples, he would not agree with the use I make of it later on.

89 "Holy Scriptures... said." Martin Luther to Frederick, Elector of Saxony, January, 1519.

91 "outshines everything. . . . modern mentality." Herbert Butterfield, *The Origins of Modern Science 1300-1800*, rev. ed. (New York: The Free Press, 1957), pp. 7-8.

"the warfare of science with theology." A.D. White, *A History of the Warfare of Science with Theology in Christendom* (New York: Apple-on, 1897) remains the classic account, from a triumphalist point of view.

92 "the state. . . hitherto known. . . . after the lapse. . . and weighed. . . .
93 nature. . . squeezed and molded." Francis Bacon, *The Great Instauration* (1620).

94 "the popular. . . preacher." Stephen Toulmin, "Scientific Theories and Scientific Myths," *The Return to Cosmology* (Berkeley: University of California Press, 1982), p. 21.

95 "The cosmos. . . ." Carl Sagan, *Cosmos* (New York: Random House, 1980), p. 4.

CHAPTER FIVE

102 "he begins. . . service to him." R.G. Collingwood, *The Idea of History* (Oxford: Oxford University Press, 1946), p. 275.

103 "that which hath. . . . subject of Story." John Milton, *The History of Britain, That part especially now called England* (1671).

110 'I had murdered. . . . am a murderer.' G.K. Chesterton, *The Secret of Father Brown* (New York: Penguin Books, 1975), pp. 11, 13.

"biography. . . enemy." Arthur James Balfour, British prime minister 1902-5, in *The London Observer*, 30 January 1927.

111 "maintained. . . extravagant superstition." Pliny, *Epistles* 10. 96.

115 "the Father. . . part of it." Tertullian, *Against Praxeas* 9.

"there was. . . Father." Tertullian, *Against Hermogenes* 3.

116 "either denying. . . divinity." Origen, *Commentary on the Gospel of John* 2. 2.

"setting aside. . . the mind." Origen, *On First Principles* 4. 4. 1.

119 "why then.... just as we have..beyond our senses.... And in a word...his being Father." Athanasius, *On the Councils of Ariminum and Seleucia* 52; 42; 49.

121 "It's a good thing I don't like broccoli...." cp. John L. Phillips, Jr., *The Origins of Intellect*, 2d ed. (San Francisco: W.H. Freeman and Company, 1975), p. 133.

'I have sent.... reply.' Lewis Carroll, preface to *Euclid and His Modern Rivals* (1879).

122 "Babies.... despised." Lewis Carroll, *Symbolic Logic: Part I. Elementary* (1896).

"the intellectual...logic." Northrop Frye, *The Great Code* (New York: Harcourt Brace Jovanovich, 1982), p. 7.

124 "It is...propositions." John Henry Newman, *An Essay in Aid of a Grammar of Assent* (1870), p. 353.

127 "the documents...light." John Henry Newman, *An Essay on the Development of Christian Doctrine* (1878), pp. 30-31.

128 "to live...often." Newman, *Christian Doctrine*, p. 40.

131 "That Jesus...it." H.E.W. Turner, *Jesus the Christ* (Oxford: Mowbray, 1976), p. 1.

"We do.... Arians." Athanasius, *Letter to Adelphius* 3.

"that Christ...redeemed." Robert C. Gregg and Dennis E. Groh, *Early Arianism—A View of Salvation* (Philadelphia: Fortress Press, 1981), p. 67.

"and lastly...mean." Athanasius, *Synodical Letter to the Bishops of Africa* 6.

"For he...divine." Athanasius, *On the Incarnation of the Son of God* 54.

132 "it leaves...modern terms." Bernard Lonergan, "The Dehellenization of Dogma," in *A Second Collection* (Philadelphia: The Westminster Press, 1974), p. 23. My interpretation of the ante-Nicene movement follows Lonergan's in *The Way to Nicea* (Philadelphia: The Westminster Press, 1976).

133 "the assumption... back to it." Leonard Hodgson, *Sex and Christian Freedom* (London: SCM Press, 1967), pp. 42-43.

CHAPTER SIX

137 Epigraph. Austin Farrer, *The Glass of Vision* (Westminster: Dacre Press, 1948), p. 41.

"Examine it.... angel." Gerald of Wales, *On the Topography of Ireland*.

140 "The Israelites... ashes.... Why... walk around it?" Frye, *The Great Code*, p. 50; pp. xviii-xix.

"has become... longer." Gordon Kaufman, "What Shall We Do With the Bible?", *Interpretation* 25 (1971):96.

144 "a piper blowing.... "Athenagoras, *Supplication for the Christians* 9.

149 "The early.... voice." Humphrey Palmer, *The Logic of Gospel Criticism* (New York: St. Martin's Press, 1968), p. 187.

150 "In re-thinking.... think it." R.G. Collingwood, *Autobiography* (New York: Penguin Books, 1944), p. 78.

152 "as of old.... pass through." Albert Schweitzer, *Geschichte der Leben-Jesu-Forschung*, 2d ed. (Tübingen: J.C.B. Mohr, 1913), p. 642.

165 "the process .. embodied in that text.... are not simply... they
166 act." Owen M. Fiss, "Objectivity and Interpretation," *Stanford Law Review* 34 (1982): 739; 745.

169 "in 1₂ ₍ₗ ual.. . canned in the canon." Krister Stendahl, "Biblical Theology, Contemporary," *Interpreter's Dictionary of the Bible*.

CHAPTER SEVEN

173 Epigraph. Richard Hooker, *Of the Laws of Ecclesiastical Polity* 5 (1597), 56.5.

177 "The characteristic . . . make things." Dorothy L. Sayers, *The Mind of the Maker* (San Francisco: Harper & Row, 1979), p. 22.

178 "How can we love . . . love God?" Augustine, *On the Trinity* 8.5.

178 "the mind . . . knowledge of itself." Augustine, *On the Trinity* 15.3.

179 "an act of love . . . society." Sayers, p. 42.

179 *Not to increase . . . His eternity.* Dante, *The Divine Comedy, Paradise*, canto 29.

181 "by the Author . . ." Sayers, p. 129.

182 *"God on the cross . . . is divine."* Friedrich Nietzsche, *The Antichrist*, in *The Portable Nietzsche*, trans. by Walter Kaufmann (New York: The Viking Press, 1954), p. 634.

182 "And by Him . . . his neighbour." W.H. Auden, "For the Time Being," in *Collected Longer Poems* (New York: Random House, 1969), p. 182.

INDEX

Cowley Publications is a work of the Society of St. John the Evangelist, a religious community for men in the Episcopal Church. The books we publish are a significant part of our ministry, together with the work of preaching, hospitality, and spiritual direction. Our aim is to provide books that will enrich their readers' religious experience as well as challenge it with fresh approaches to religious concerns.

M. Thomas Shaw, SSJE